EATING FOR ENERGY

EATING FOR ENERGY

eating five healthy nutritious meals a day gives you energy to get you going throughout the day

STEVE EDMOND

authorHOUSE®

AuthorHouse™
1663 Liberty Drive
Bloomington, IN 47403
www.authorhouse.com
Phone: 1-800-839-8640

First published by AuthorHouse   10/31/2011

ISBN: 978-1-4670-6465-1 (sc)
ISBN: 978-1-4670-6464-4 (ebk)

Library of Congress Control Number: 2011918426

Printed in the United States of America

About The Author

Readers who chose this book will be very intreged to find out that this book which was written by steve edmond was made to be easy for all to understand. Originally steve was an inspired natural bodybuilder male fitness model who competed in all national level shows while traveling all over the united states. He also took up the study of nutrition at a local community college in charles town massachussettes all while working as a personal trainer in the heart of down town Boston. in the mean time steve really enjoyed training other people and helping them to achieve their physical goals while making them feel great about them selves including writing nutrition regimens for his clients and non clients. One day on his free time he was going through his desk at work and found that he had written so many nutrition regimens that he had enough information to write a book. As time went by a lot was going through his mind. He thought to himself, what if i could pass my knowledge on to a wider audience and get the message across that way, what about the possability of having my own book published for the public to read? Then the idea came to life which is now what you are holding in your hands. Steve edmond was born in orlando florida and is the fith child out of eight kids. Growing up wasn't as hard for him although he didn't have the luxerury of being spoiled by his parents. His parent who are originally of carrabien decent came to the united states for a better way of life and to take care of steve and his siblings made sure that he had food on the table every night and clean clothes on his back. In highschool steve was involved in many different sports but his most favorite was American footbal, baseball and indoor track. Just like most young men, steve was more of the skinny kid but he was athletic and fast. It wasn't until one day while practicing, his coach told him that he needed to put some size on if he ever wanted to take the sport of football any further. and so he did. as time went on steve began taking a liking to weight lifting because he noticed that his body was going through a change going from skinny to muscular in a matter of eight months. Before long the idea of him continueing on to play sports just took a back seat and he stuck to the weights. To make a long story short, one of steves friends was reading a muscle magazine and in that magazine was an advertizement detailing an up and coming local bodybuilding show. It took some time to talk him into entering the show but he finally did. the first show didn't go so well for him because it was his first one which he also didn't do well at all. but he never gave up and kept right at it. After doing a string of other bodybuilding shows and winning a few titles, he found himself a new hobby. and that's how today he is known by many of his friends as a bodybuilder and a person to come to for nutrition and exercise information.

What is Eating for Energy?

What I told you that you could increase your energy to a consistent level throughout your day, week, and lifetime? Wouldn't you rather have the choices you make help you to thrive, instead of merely survive?

In today's busy world, the importance of healthy eating can become less and less of a priority for some people. Fast food drive thrus, energy drinks, skipping meals, and lack of exercise have become habits that people have fallen into and may not even be aware of.

Eating for Energy discusses some of these habits and much more, showing you a better way to maintain a healthy body weight, increase energy levels, and prevent illnesses and diseases by promoting clean eating.

Arming your with the information you need to stay committed to healthy eating at home, at work, and even dining out, *Eating for Energy* is your handbook for a healthier, stronger, more energetic life.

Chapter 1

Eating for a Lifetime

Insuring that you can continue to live, you have to eat. Food is the body's version of fuel. The important thing that you need to make sure to follow up on is to make sure that you are eating healthy foods so that you don't simply live your life, but also live a healthy life.

Eating healthy is a building block for foundation of a healthy body. This is a habit that should begin from the time of early childhood and should continue to the time you have reached old age. Eating nutrient rich foods makes a difference on how you feel each day and also in the long term.

In this chapter, we will be talking about how to come up with a healthy diet for you and also enough information that you have learned and might want to pass on to your friends and family.

Why Food is Important

The reason why we need food is because it is what helps us grow, gives us energy, and keeps us alive. Foods, such as whole wheat bread, apples, or ice cream contain at least two main categories of nutrients: macronutrients and micronutrients. They are required in a large amount for helping you to develop and grow properly. Both macronutrients and micronutrients from the basis of every diet, providing energy for the body and all activities that lie ahead. Macronutrients are considered to be primarily carbohydrates, fat, or fiber. Most foods in general contain all of these categories, but in varying proportions.

Micronutrients are a makeup of vitamins and minerals and are types of chemical compounds that can be found in tiny amounts of foods, which is not the case for macronutrients. Vitamins and minerals in micronutrients are needed, because they play a very important role in the body's functions and digestive system.

Although some people tend to eat much healthier foods than others, it turns out that we all eat a wide range of different foods everyday from different food groups, which provides many nutrients. The problem is not everyone eats the right nutrient rich foods.

Your Changing Food Preferences

Everyone goes through different stages of their lives when bodies start to change. As a baby, you are expected to take in a lot of foods that are rich in nutrients for proper growth, strong bones and teeth, and good health. By the time you reach well into your teenage years, the diet intake changes. Sometimes, problems may consist of varying from not eating enough food throughout the day to eating the wrong foods. Good healthy food intake is something that should be continued on throughout life, but yet most do not follow this habit.

One thing that you should know is that it is never too late to start. If you have kids of your own, then now would be a perfect time to teach them what they too should know so that knowledge can be passed on to their kids and so on.

Taking in proper nutrition has a major impact on a child's health in a good way, promoting normal growth, development, and limits long-term health consequences by the time they are adults.

By providing healthy, nutritious foods for your child, you are giving them what is important for their child's growth throughout childhood. It's important to ensure that he or she is taking in enough calories and the proper nutrients, avoiding childhood obesity, adult obesity, or being malnourished.

THE BEGINNING OF GOOD EATING HABITS

It is very important that good eating habits are introduced to young children for contributing good health and maintaining their correct body weight from childhood into adulthood.

Being a good role model for your child is one sure way to get them to want to live a healthy lifestyle, making it much easier for them by the time they are older. Other effective ways of introducing your child to healthy eating is to have family sit down meals as much as possible. And, also, when it comes to snacks, everyone knows that a child will be less likely to turn it down, especially if it has to do with something sweet and fattening. They may not know how unhealthy that snack is, but an adult in their life will. Their role models should really consider making that choice of introducing a wide variety of healthy snacks for them to choose—without forcing them. Make things fun for them by mixing fruits or vegetables in fun and exciting ways.

One thing that seems to get kids' taste buds going is color. The more color there is to the variety, the better chance there is of an empty container, which is what you or any parent would want. When you give your child a healthy wide range of snacks to eat, it will give them plenty of energy to go throughout the day.

You should also pack their school lunch boxes with a nutrient rich lunch. Also, keep them active by cutting their television time, video game play, and computer time. You should also limit their consumption of junk foods and unhealthy drinks, which can be very high in calories, which are part of the reason for excessive weight gain and obesity if not consumed in small moderations.

Besides you learning about what foods are good for you, you should also teach your child about food as well. It is important that the child knows the difference between healthy foods that are good for you and junk foods that are hazardous to your health. Not to mention, it's necessary to teach them that whatever they eat and drink plays a role in what their future will be like. After all, haven't you heard the saying, "You are what you eat"?

Eating at the Right Time

Some of us go through life surrounded by environmental distractions that condition our eating patterns. For example, working late and not having lunch during the day because you were probably too busy. But, by the time you got home, you were hungry, causing you to want to have a late night snack and sit in front of the television set until you fell asleep.

This habit is best known as an eating script, because it's a routine witch exerts bad effects on consumption. Unfortunately, we are sometimes aware of them. There are jobs out there that have become more fast paced, and new scripts have emerged that may seem more conductive. Many men can feel driven by this. More often, they tend to either skip daytime meals entirely or relegate them to refuel as soon as possible.

Almost one third of men, compared to a quarter of women, admit to eating fast food all the time. This can cause obesity. Obesity is also caused by skipping breakfast and substituting it with not so healthy snacks. This is why it causes men to put on excess amounts of unhealthy weight.

You must be able to recognize your food weakness and then correct your behavior. Start bringing lunch from home, such as a grilled chicken sandwich topped with a spoon of low-fat mayonnaise, lettuce, tomatoes, one slice of low-fat American cheese and wheat bread. Or a turkey wrap with cranberry relish. This can also help you to avoid a drive thru.

Keep up this experiment until you can find healthy foods that you can live with. If you want to have a sugar glazed doughnut, then go ahead and have it. But, remember, you must have at least a piece of fruit or some veggies first, and then see how much of a craving you might have for that glazed doughnut. More often than not, your craving will subside, and you will choose healthier options.

Why Healthy Eating is Important

There are many good reasons of why you should be eating healthy.

1.) Eating healthy can help make you feel good.

2.) It is the key to helping you look good.

3.) Three, full course, healthy meals, ranging from breakfast, lunch, and dinner as well as a healthy snack in between can help the body prevent itself from developing diseases, such as cardiovascular disease, and diabetes.

4.) Eating a healthy meal may not only help you to be healthy but also maintain it too.

5.) Eating healthy gives you plenty of energy. After all, the body relies on good healthy eating habits for getting and making the energy that it needs.

6.) Another reason why eating a healthy nutritious balanced meal every day is it may help to bring your body fat percentage down to where it needs to be.

7.) Eating healthy may add more years to your life span and make you happy, live happy, and feel better about yourself too.

Improving Your Health

A lot of people may not know this, but quite a few of them actually care about the foods they eat. However, the types of foods you eat are very important for determining what your health is going to be like for the future and how it is now. In this chapter, we will be reviewing how important it is to eating healthy and how that can help prevent future health problems. Even if you currently suffer from certain disorders, now would be a good time to start.

The good part is that there are people who seem to want to gain more knowledge in health, especially if it has to do with preventing them from getting sick. After all, no one likes being sick or suffering from health complications. Eating healthy along with getting plenty of exercise can actually help fight off diseases, such as cancer, cardiovascular disease, osteoporosis, and diabetes.

Eating healthy throughout your life is a sure way to ensure that you live a happy and disease free life. But keep following a diet that is high in bad fats and low in nutrients, and you are more likely to develop clogged arteries and other life threatening disorders.

A healthy, consistent diet of highly nutritious food can help the body treat health related problems. However, few people in the United States are developing cardiovascular disease these days, due to our reduction of consuming bad, fatty foods.

Although people in the U.S. are limiting their fat intake, they are still doing more eating and less exercising, causing more of them to be obese. The more weight that a person gains, the more of a risk they have of developing cardiovascular disease.

This is why it is very important to balance healthy eating with portion size and exercise so that the risk of developing such diseases is reduced.

Making Good Food Choices

The key to living a better, healthy life is to make better food choices that are rich in nutrients. It may not happen overnight, but it can be done. Gradually, that is, you can accomplish your goals.

These foods include products that are rich in fiber and also contain complex carbohydrates. Compounds that are high in fiber and complex carbohydrates are a lot better than foods that are high in sugar. When a food compound is high in fiber, it usually digests slower, which is important for the energy that the body needs so that it can be slowly released. This is a negative for highly sugary foods, which will only give off quick energy to the body before finally bringing the energy levels back down just as fast as you got it.

Not just having a salad here and there and then drowning the lettuce in dressing is going to cut it. It may even require some low-fat salad dressing instead of regular. At first, things may feel a little odd, but don't push yourself into a clean diet right away. For example, let's just say you are not a fan of vegetables, and your doctor tells you that your blood pressure is high, recommending that you start adding vegetables to your diet. Then the best thing to do would be to add little pieces of vegetables to your dinner every night and slowly bring up the portions. Believe me, after a while you might get so used to eating greens that it becomes second nature.

Whenever you go food shopping, you may not notice, but the majority of the things that you put in your food basket you don't really need. Instead, get used to eating healthy so that that you began to love the flavor.

Considering eating junk food and fast food as an addiction, you have to gradually wean yourself from poor eating habits and food choices If you stop while you are food shopping and take the time to read the back of the label of what you are planning to buy, it will amaze you. The total amount of fat and calorie content that are hidden in these meals is astonishing.

Something that you should know is that you don't really need to give up all your favorite foods. This is simply because they all have substitutes or fat-free versions that are sold right beside the normal packages too. Sometimes being picky can be a good thing, just as long as you choose to do it at the right time, for the right reasons, and at the right places. After all, this is the beginning of a healthy start. And also the smart way for keeping track of what you are putting into your body.

Chapter 2

Weight Control for Energy

Almost every person has a certain weight they would like to be at or a certain way they would like to look. Controlling your weight can make you look and feel better. Not only that, but it can also help the average person decrease their risk of developing medical problems in the future, such as high blood pressure, diabetes, cardio vascular disease, high blood cholesterol, and even cancer.

Most people, at times, don't even think of this, and if they do, their thoughts are usually fleeting. Maybe it is time to start looking at weight control as a more serious matter. Weight control doesn't mean to go on an eating strike; it just means that all you have to do is bring the body weight to the point that it is right for you. By doing this, you will basically be improving your appearance and health. Weight control is even important for the current and future of your life. It sure doesn't pay to be overweight, let me tell you.

Your weight should be a perfect match for what your height is. However, finding the right strategy that will work for you is really the most important thing. Not only do you need to find the perfect strategy that will work, but also, you should have one for the long term.

Don't be fooled by diets that swear up and down that you will see quick results. Yes, they may work in the beginning, while things are still fresh, but these diets are not suitable in the long run for controlling your weight. After a while, your body begins to not respond to the diets that are supposed to be delivering quick results, which is known as a set point, or plateau. This is where the body starts to defend the weight it is at. Rather than falling into something like this, stick to regular exercise, such as walking, jogging, weight lifting, or jump roping.

When you consume a lot of calories for a short time, the body uses them by creating more heat. But, if you end up using more calories than you consume, the body is more likely to become more efficient at converting the calories into energy. Thus, it prevents short term weight loss.

When someone has that goal of wanting to lose weight or gain it, they have to take that goal seriously enough for those achievements to be met. You have to ask yourself, where would you start? Honestly saying you want to gain or lose weight is much easier said than done. Not only that, but it is also much easier to get discouraged when one doesn't see results.

THE BENEFITS OF WEIGHT CONTROL

Controlling your weight so that it is just right for you is one of the main keys to your health. Remember, when a person is overweight, they are putting themselves at risk for developing a lot of health problems, which also means their lifespan is shortened.

Losing weight can help benefit your life. In addition to the benefits of living a healthier, longer life, losing up to 10% of extra unwanted weight can actually lower your blood pressure and also reduce the risk of developing cardiovascular disease or even suffer a stroke.

Losing weight can also lower blood cholesterol and triglyceride levels, which are what causes the development of cardiovascular disease. Being overweight just does not pay off at all, at least not from the health point of view. An overweight person is more likely to develop Type-2 diabetes than people who carefully maintain healthy body weight. In addition to losing weight, it also decreases the risk of developing diabetes and reduces blood glucose levels. It can also reduce the other risk of developing osteoarthritis. by taking the stress off your joints, such as the lower spine, hips, and knees.

These parts of the body are usually what are already more affected by osteoarthritis. When an overweight person looks into having surgery for replacing arthritic joint, hips, and knees, they would be advised to lose weight before going through with the process. Controlling their weight is important so that the surgery can be successful.

Being overweight and obese, are part of the major reasons for cancer, which includes (for women) cervix, ovary, gallbladder, breast, uterus, and colon. For men, these cancers may include rectum, prostate, and colon. Another reason why losing weight is so important is because it will also reduce the risk of all the above.

Being overweight can cause many other health related problems, such as sleep apnea. Sleep apnea is a condition that is accompanied with this problem. Weight reduction can help improve sleep apnea.

For some people, losing weight can seem like an obstacle too big to accomplish. Actually, weight reduction is something that anybody can do, just as long as they choose to eat the right foods and include exercise. They, too, will be able to achieve this goal.

Everyone responds to certain diets differently. Some people may lose more weight than others, depending on how serious they take their regimen. Even the slightest amount of weight loss will help lower blood pressure and reduce the risk for cardiovascular disease. Controlling your weight and keeping it steady enhances self esteem and health in addition to overall appearance.

Choosing the Right Diet for You

There are a lot of diets out there that claim to be good for weight loss. However, not all of them work for everyone the same way. Weight loss is something that a lot of us have tried to do at one point or another, depending on what the reason was for. Some of us were probably so desperate to get whatever weight we could off that we looked for the fastest way possible.

Weight loss is now considered to be a million dollar project industry, ranging from gyms and diet books to weight loss programs, foods, and medications dedicated for those people looking to lose weight. The bad news is when the weight does come off quickly; it ends up being packed back on twice as fast, causing nothing but frustration. If this situation sounds familiar because it has happened to you, well now is the time to think about finding a diet plan that is going to work for the long term.

Weight loss isn't easy, and there is no easy way to do it. If you think you have found an easier, faster way, then chances are, you are doing it wrong. In order to lose unwanted weight and keep it off, it takes time and dedication to do it right and succeed.

To tell you the truth, I can remember countless times when I would be sitting in my living room on an early Saturday morning, and all I can remember seeing was some commercial advertisement on television about some so-called, new abdominal machine or some so-called, new and improved Hollywood juice diet. The quick results it promised is what a lot of people want to hear, but what many of them don't realize is that most of the people shown on television are just actors that are already in shape, simply hired to use and promote the machines and products to giving viewers hope.

Choosing the right diet is not easy either. This is a transition that doesn't happen overnight, regardless of what type of weight loss diet you choose. However, there will always be guidelines that are there to help you succeed in the ways of changing your diet habits.

Try avoiding being around unhealthy foods, where you know the consumption is likely to occur. Avoid skipping out on meals. Stop eating late at night. The best way to avoid doing this is to start going to bed earlier. And, another thing that you should do is stop rewarding yourself at the end of the week with cheat meals.

Once you began doing this, it will lead to over-consumption of junk food, which is pointless. Before getting on any type of diet plan, you should speak to your doctor or nutritionist even if and when certain supplements or medications are involved. This is always better, because you can always be well monitored. You can even monitor yourself by checking your weight and seeing how well you progress, preferably once a week.

By going over nutrition, supplements, and medications with your doctor or nutritionist, they can help you determine what is best for you. Again, you may also be advised to take vitamins and minerals. No vitamin, mineral, or supplement should be taken by anyone under the age of 18. Remember, there is not one diet out there that can be the best way for everyone to lose weight. The majority of weight loss diets work for some people, but not for everyone. As you experiment with diet after diet, you will soon learn what works for you and what doesn't.

In addition, there are many varieties of diets. Some of them have limited macronutrients, such as carbohydrates and fat, while others may limit foods, such as starchy carbohydrates. Some people concentrate on foods, such as fruits, like grapefruit, or vegetables. Others may just simply concentrate on diets that are 30 percent fat, 30 percent protein and 40 percent carbohydrates.

FIGHTING AGAINST OBESITY

Back in the year 2000, the U.S. surgeon general had reported that obesity had topped the epidemic proportions; at least half of the adults in the U.S and a quarter of American children were overweight. This still is the case today. This is something that happened over the last 22 years. There are many ways to change and control your weight.

Of course a lot of people that are obese do not enjoy being that way. They even know how many health risks are involved. Being obese can kill a person. The more overweight a person is, the greater the risk they have of developing certain diseases and dying early.

Not only is being excessively overweight bad for the health, but it also puts a lot of strain on the back, heart, joints, and organs. It can even cause high blood pressure and cardio vascular disease as well. Obesity has also been known to cause osteoarthritis, respiratory disease, and gallstones.

Reducing Junk Food Intake

Developing a way to reduce snacks and junk food is the first step in fighting against obesity and maintaining a healthy body weight. With goals of healthy weight management and eating, one should learn to master, it's important to note that the majority of snacks out there that are not healthy can, in fact, contain relatively high calories, sodium, and carbohydrates.

I understand how it feels to be super hungry, because, just like you, I get hunger cravings too. There are times when hunger strikes, and your cravings give you the desire to want to eat anything.

What I have learned to do is to carry a healthy snack with me wherever I went, such as a piece of fruit or raw, unsalted almonds. Whenever I got hungry, I would snack on them.

I made sure that I had enough to carry me throughout the day for whenever I got hungry between breakfast, lunch, and dinner. This method is good for preventing room for the consumption of junk food.

When you are hungry and need a snack, try going for something healthy like fruits or vegetables. To some, these types of snacks can be a bit boring. If you end up feeling this way at times, then feel free to mix things up a bit with other healthy foods.

Do some research on what other healthy foods might be available to choose from, specifically varieties that are good for having in between meals. This is also good for even when you choose to snack during the times that you are bored. Try finding out what situations trigger the problem of wanting to consume unhealthy snacks. Find different strategies that will work. For example, go for a walk or read a book or magazine. Even when you do go for a walk, avoid taking routes where you know you will bump in to the restaurants or small corner stores.

To make sure that this works, bring a bottle of water with you to sip on. When cravings start to happen, you can just sip in the water until the end of your walk back home. Also, leave your money and credit and debit cards at home. You will be surprised to find out how well this procedure works when you try to cheat on your strategy.

I know you might be thinking of this as something more suitable to avoiding overspending. Yes, but this method is also good for keeping you from getting distracted or buying and eating the wrong foods.

When you buy a food item, check its ingredients on the package, if the sugar is listed as high as 19—29, more than likely that food is high in calories, and it will even contain very little nutritional value. You basically don't need all the sugar. The less you have, the better it is.

If you find it hard to be able to stay away from sugar, try retraining your taste buds by aiming to eat less sugary foods, such as candy bars, tonic beverages, like coke and other soda, and even sugary deserts.

For some people, this goal might require a little more concentration to avoid discouragement. When planning to work at a goal, such as weight control, it can be quite a bit of a challenge.

TROUBLESHOOTING THE CHALLENGES OF WEIGHT LOSS

Changing your eating habits for controlling your body weight is not something that can be done overnight, but it can be gradually and with dedication. If you happen to be the one who suffers from being overweight and want to make this goal accomplishable, even if you find it extremely difficult to begin or control your weight, you must not give up. For example, start off by cutting out certain foods that you know will prevent you from bringing unwanted body weight down.

The way to succeeding weight control is to balance how many calories you take in with how many you burn up in the course of the daily activities. Try not to eat more than you need, doing so will only be stored as fat because of the excess calories. Keep active. The more exercise that you do, the more food you can take in. This enables you to maintain healthy weight. Remember, the plan here is to eat healthy foods to meet the goal of weight control.

Eat plenty of fruits and vegetables. Fruits and vegetables are packed with vitamins and minerals, and they are usually low in calories. Fruits and vegetables are also important because when you are cutting back on excess weight, there is a limited amount of calories that you can consume in a day if your goal is to lose or maintain weight.

Try taking in at least two servings of vegetables with a meal. This is also a trick to helping to fill you up, reducing your desire to snack on non-healthy foods. Instead, if you eat a banana or two or maybe an orange about an hour before eating a regular meal, you will be more likely to eat less when the time comes to eat. Stay away from foods that are high in fats; they contain large amounts of calories and carbohydrates, which is a sure way to cause failure of not meeting your goals.

If you want to feel satisfied with cutting calories and still be full, avoid eating fatty foods. (Although in this book, I mention that you should be use olive oil or other healthy cooking oils when cooking, they still should be used more cautiously and with limited use. Even healthy cooking oils contain 100 calories per tablespoon.)

Take it easy on the fried foods as well. Instead, switch to baked or grilled foods, which are much better for you health wise. Remember, almost every fatty food out there has an alternative to it. Choose to eat healthy, and look forward to your new, healthy future.

STRATEGIES FOR MAINTAINING A HEALTHY DIET

Just like I have mentioned earlier in this book, in order to begin losing weight, you have to eat foods that contain less calories and add plenty of exercise into the mix to get the ball rolling. Now, remember, when consuming foods with fewer calories, you still have to make sure that you are still getting lots of nutrients. Take your time. Always choose what you eat carefully. For example, only eat foods that are highly nutritious, but low in calories. Avoid an intake of high calorie and low nutrient foods, such as sugary snacks, like cookies, candy, soda, and even chips. Throughout the rest of this chapter, there will be some examples to give you an idea on what to do as far as helping you put together a well balanced healthy diet that will help you lose weight and stay healthy. For each day, you should have three servings of vegetables, because they are a perfect, valuable source of phytochemicals that are good for your health and are also low in calories.

For more nutrients out of vegetables, it is better to eat some of them raw. If you choose to cook them, which most do taste better cooked, find healthier ways, such as microwaving or steaming them. Do not add cheese, butter, or any unhealthy alternatives. Doing this will just defeat the purpose. You can also use a small amount of olive oil, vegetable spray, or even canola oil.

Do not forget the fruits. Try having two servings between meals or when hungry. Fruits can also make a great snack to have anytime during the day or for desert.

When you are on a serious weight loss regimen, you should also consider watching out for preservatives. Instead, try eating whole grain breads. These have more fiber, which can fill you up better. It is also good to eat grains for breakfast and anytime during the day. Also throw some vegetables in there to help change up the eating routine every now and then.

Sometimes, a little bit of legumes here and there for added protein works too, which is vital for the body's needs. Speaking of protein, dairy products are a must have. Dairy is good to add into the mix, because they help promote weight loss, not weight gain. The higher that the calcium intake is, the better of a chance you have at succeeding in losing weight.

It is important to choose fat-free or low-fat dairy products. No matter what a person's tolerance for dairy is, most can consume some type of dairy products. Preferably dairy that contains lactase enzyme, which is much safer for those who cannot hold up well with the regular variety.

Other good sources of protein that you should remember to add are regular meat varieties. The goal here isn't to eat red meat all the time or regular meat in general; there are other sources that you can obtain protein from, which was mentioned earlier in this chapter. Instead, mix these different varieties up each day so that you are not bored enough to discontinue your plans of weight loss. Choose sources that are low in saturated fats, such as eggs, fish, soy products, white skinless chicken, or lean cut meats.

TELEVISION TRIGGERS

I don't know what it is, but did you know that seeing food on television can trigger a physiological response, such as the body wanting to be fed, even when you've probably ate, hmm, let's see, an hour ago?

Food cues can cause the brain activities to jump by 24 percent, mostly in the part of the brain called the orbito frontal cortex. This can mean a constant food commercial that keeps showing pizza, burgers, or whatever type of food that is shown on television could really test your limits.

THE POWER OF PORTION CONTROL

For some, knowing your limits is half the battle. Knowing when you're full and knowing when to stop can make all the difference in your weight loss goals. Here are some simple steps to keep your portions under contol.

1.) Choose a smaller-sized plate.

Make it a habit of downsizing your mealtime plates. To do so you must first get rid of all your oversized ones and invest in a 16 piece set. These usually come with six 10.5 inch plates, four six inch salad plates, and a four7 inch soup bowls.

Instead of choosing to eat off of the larger plate, choose the salad plate. It will help you to eat smaller portions and still feel like you've eaten a full plate of food.

2.) Stock up on 100-calorie snack packs.

If you are a person who loves to snack, then the next time you go to the supermarket, grab yourself a box of 100-calorie snack packs. The best thing about it is that there are plenty of selections to choose from.

3.) Eat half of your food; then, wait.

Keep in mind that another good way to lessen your food serving is to eat half of your food and then wait 10 minutes before going back for a second serving.

Try to spark up a conversation with your friends and sip on some water. Doing so will give your stomach a chance to digest. By then, your tummy might decide whether you've had enough.

4.) Choose smaller containers of food instead of the "family size" ones.

The sizes of the container from which you buy your food can have an impact on how much we eat. Instead of choosing a "family size" can, jar, or package of food, choose the regular size instead. A small can of soup may not seem like enough food, but you may find that it is. If you start small, you can always add more later. But if you start big, you may find yourself eating more than is necessary.

You have to be able to make good decisions and make a change for yourself. Doing so can help you lose up to 10-15 pounds, maybe more, depending on your goals and on how motivated you are.

KICKING UP THE METABOLISM

I have a theory that goes like this: if you are able to drop 5 pounds, you can lose some more. Just imagine if you keep up the pace, stick to your goals, and change up exercises every few weeks as well as steering clear of unhealthy foods. Trust and believe me, you'll transform your physique into a lean, mean fighting machine. Who knows, maybe by next summer, you'll probably have long met your goals. Whether it is to look good for an up and coming trip to Cancun, or simply just to be healthy while looking good at the same time, whatever your goal is, just by getting a few pointers and ideas from this book, you will be covered in the sense that you will know what to eat or not eat.

Sometimes, the closer you get to what you want your weight to be is when your fat stores become stubborn. This is natural, expect it to happen. Some people have more fat stores than others, due to the body being designed to protect your fuel reserves. For example, let's say maybe you get stranded somewhere and food was hard to come by.

Well, guess what? I believe that, if I can do it, so can you. Here is the trick to help kick up your metabolism: Exercise. This is something that should be done to get that flat six pack midsection that you are hiding underneath. But you can't achieve anything if you do not put in any effort and dedication.

Chapter 3

Exercising for Energy

The key to succeeding with your goals of maintaining a healthy body weight is to balance what you eat with exercise, and the energy it provides, with the amount of energy you use in the course of your life.

The Last 10 Pounds

I am going to keep it real with you. No matter what type of exercise and movement you do, you'll always sort of hit a plateau on how much fat you lose during a 30 to 35 minute workout. The efficiency of your body improves over time as it becomes well trained, burning fewer calories.

If you are a runner, the best way to avoid weight gain, especially when aging, is to bring up your weekly mileage up to 1.8 miles a year.

When trying to get rid of the last ten pounds, do not panic. Put some thought into how you plan on getting it done.

Concentrate when working out. Keep track of how much you burn during the day as you sit on your butt, sleep, or chill on the couch in front of your television set, and compare that to how much you can burn when engaged in physical activity.

Remember, this isn't going to happen with a quick snap of the finger. It's going to have to take weights, cardio, and clean eating to get to where you want to be, look, and health wise. This chapter will help you to stack on track with tips for finding the right cardio, exercise regimen, reps, and how long to rest in between sets, this too will help you burn calories with fat burning hormones, which can keep your metabolism burning like Mount St. Helens'.

THE TOTAL BODY WORKOUT

Working out using weights or exercising the entire body is relatively a great way to ensure that the metabolism gets a boost on fat burning. What matters is how you make create your workouts and the different parts of muscle groups you activate. It is best to work with movements that focus on these muscles to isolate each group. For example, say you want to focus on doing squats; for that, you should do for repetitions of 10. Compare this to the ten repetitions of an isolated exercise of doing biceps curls. Just by you training the entire body every time you workout, you'll get to hit every muscle in your body.

Based on the study from the University of Wisconsin, if you were to do a full body workout including squats, bench press, and power clean, your metabolism would be lifted as much as 39 hours after, while burning a lot of calories during the process. Compare yourself to a guy who didn't train his entire body and see what the difference is.

So the next time you go to the gym, try to remember if bench today, do another body part tomorrow. Or you can do the total body workout by training three days a week and rest one day in between the days you workout. Doing this is a sure way to keep your metabolism as high as a Ferraris revs 24/7.

Strength Training to Boost Your Metabolism

When training and going for a set, you should be doing 10 to 15 repetitions. Doing anything less than that, you'll only end up looking like one of the strongmen from the strong man competition, which isn't what we are aiming for. Instead, we do want to be strong and fit. The goal is to pump out reps for burning. Doing 10 to 15 repetitions increases stimulation in fat burning hormones, which is the opposite of what doing fewer repetitions can deliver, like, let's just say, a number range of 6 to 8 repetitions. Now, don't go thinking that you are going to go through this the easy way buy picking up little five pound weights.

However, do use weights that you can handle, allowing you to get ten good reps. If you happen to struggle during your last rep, then that is a sign that you have picked the right weight to train with. Avoid heavy weights to prevent injury. You want your muscles to produce 100% of work, doing full reps, for full range of motion, not half.

The Importance of Well-Planned Sets

Regardless of what type of exercise, when working out, you should do at least 2 to 4 sets for each type that you choose. Do not go crazy. Going beyond this mark is just not worth it. After all, just after a set or two, your fat burning hormones increase. When starting off from the beginning, this should be the range of numbers you stay at. Depending on your condition of status, then you could go up in sets as your body begins to ask for more.

Alternating in between sets is another way of promising your body to help it burn fat. Not only that, but switching from exercise to exercise also stops you from engaging in conversations with the other people. Keep sets and reps coming one after another. Then continue on into sets that lead you into working muscles that were not being worked on during other movements. Repeat this process until you are done. When training like this, you are actually performing alternating sets, which allows a group of muscles to rest as the other group goes to work, keeping the lactate levels high as certain muscles get more time to rest between sets. The point to doing this is to prevent fatigue and help you train with substantial effort every time you perform a set.

You want to work each and every muscle hard enough on every repetition you do on each set. Do not forget: take your time. Use control when lifting. Without jerking or rocking back and forth, raise the weight and lower back to position slowly. You never want to do any exercise too fast, because you end can up taking the stress off of the muscles that you are working on and cause injury.

Injury is what prevents the metabolism from burning fat. The rule to lifting weights is to try to lower the weight and count for 3 seconds; then pause for a second before continuing to the next set. Doing this prevents you from cheating, giving your muscles the chance to work hard.

As important as it is to plan your sets, resting in between sets and the amount of time spend doing so is just as important. When resting in between sets, you should be resting for around 70 to 80 seconds. Depending on what your energy levels are like, between sets, possibly less time can be allowed for resting. Avoid going to the gym to socialize or using that time as a chance to read your newspaper to check out the stock market or sports. There is a time and place for that.

Here is a hint: the less rest you have by keeping your body physically active, the more of a chance you have to speed up the fat loss process. For example, when doing 10 to 15 reps in an exercise, the accumulation of a chemical known as lactate in your blood stream occurs. This is associated with the increased release of fat burning hormones. You do not want to rest for too long because the oxygen you take in will eventually clear the lactate from the bloodstream. This is why you should limit how long you rest between each set: to keep fat burning hormones high and burning more fat as you rest.

THE KEY TO THE NEXT LEVEL: CARDIO

Although cardiovascular and any type of exercise that involves aerobics helps the body to burn calories, it isn't always necessary to do it if you are already a clean eater. If not, then please continue on.

Cardiovascular exercise is part of the finishing touch to bringing out those rock hard abs from hibernation. If I told you this, you might not believe me, but running long distances should be left for if you feel the need to train for the Boston Marathon, which still isn't a bad idea then. You don't have to run long distances to burn calories, because it doesn't do too much to bring fat loss to another level. If you think aerobics exercise boosts fat loss, think again.

Now don't take this as a free ticket out of doing cardiovascular. The best thing to help you boost your metabolism is doing high intensity, 35-second sprints, mixed with some slow jogging, which help to promote fat loss. Consider this technique: to be the brother of weight lifting, they are both physical activities that challenge the body from every angle. Also try doing this on days you are not weight training. This is the next key to boosting your metabolism to the next level.

A Quick Guide to Sweat

When doing any type of cardio or other exercise, it's always best to work up a good sweat. You know that your body is working hard if you're sweating. You should never be embarrassed about sweating. It is good for you, because it helps to regulate the body's temperature.

Additionally, sweating is important because it helps prevent E.I.A, which stands for Exercise Induced Asthma. Exercise induced asthma can effect athletes and the exercises that they do. In addition to sweat being able to keep the body cool when it overheats, it also prevents the body from developing E.I.A.

When an athlete has E.I.A, they produce less tears, saliva, and sweat than regular people who do not have breathing problems. People who do not sweat as much have drier air ways, which can cause problems with the respiratory system.

In order for an athlete with this problem to prevent things from getting worse, they would have to control the quality of air while working out and pay attention to their intake of liquids and nutrition. This also helps to reduce hyperactive airways.

Unfortunately, many don't know about the good qualities that sweat have, and instead, many people can find sweating disgusting, mainly because of the bad odor that it creates. I do have to admit, sometimes, you can really stink, especially when working out or during hot climates. However, everyone has different odors that their body gives off when they sweat.

Sweat is made up of water, salt potassium, chloride, and sodium as well as other bodily mixtures. A person has about 2.6 million sweat glands in the skin, primarily over the entire body. The body consists of two types of sweat glands: one of them is apocrine and the other eccrine. Apocrine produce really a small amount of thick fluid from the body that is basically odorless, and eccrine produce the more watery part of the sweat.

Our bodies are also covered with eccrine glands, which are included on foreheads, palms of hands, and the soles of the feet. While the apocrine glands are located under the arms and in the genital area, the glands that are located under it are also apocrine glands.

When bodies release this thick odorless sweat from the apocrine glands, it sits on the skin, which then causes the bacteria to react, which gives the body a really fou smell. This gland contains fatty acids and proteins that make the secretion thicker and milky-like, giving it a buttery color. This is why whenever you are at the gym and you happen to be wearing a white t-shirt, the sweat from your under arm appears to be yellowish in color. People do not develop apocrine glands until they reach puberty, which is why most never worry about smelly armpits until they get older.

However, men lose more sweat through their bodies than women do. Some people can actually handle hot days better than others, due to them sweating a lot when exercising all year round. This makes them more acclimated in the spring and able to handle the hot summer days or hot climate that they may be living in better. However, when a person has not been in a hot climate for a long time, they end up producing one liter of sweat an hour. After six weeks, the body will start to adjust, producing two or three liters of sweat.

Did you know that the population of people in the United States who suffer from hyperuidrosis is 3 percent? This is true. Hyperuidrosis is known as excessive sweating, which affect the underarms, hands, and feet. It is also known to happen when the weather is bitterly cold.

No matter what people say, everyone sweats, even when you can't see it. But, pay attention, and look at your fingers. There you will see little beads of sweat, or you may find some even off the top of your nose. This is caused by the humidity of air that surrounds you. This also affects the way that the sweat evaporates when the humidity is high. Air absorption is impossible, making the moisture and sweat unable to evaporate and cool the body. When you lose a lot of sweat, you get very easily dehydrated; this causes problems, such as kidney failure and heat stroke.

There are safety precautions that you should take when working out. Some of these precautions include not wearing so many layers of clothing or not wearing a plastic sweat suit, especially on really hot, muggy days. Although you will, in fact, lose plenty of water weight, you won't lose many calories. Layering clothing to produce excessive sweating is unhealthy and can lead to heat stroke.

Sweat is made up of fluids in the blood. The more sweat you lose, the thicker the blood gets, making your heart work harder in order to pump blood through the body. The more physically fit you are, the better it is for you to deal with low or moderate degrees of dehydration than people who are not.

When you go running for a long period of time, it is best to drink around 12 to 16 ounces of water. Soon after, preferably about every 15 to 20 minutes, drink 6 to 12 ounces while exercising, running, or in between sets of workouts.

Staying hydrated is an essential part of working out. Without adequate rest time and a time to replenish with water the sweat and energy that your body has used, you will not be working out as efficiently each time you begin your exercise routine.

Stay motivated and remain dedicated to keeping off that unwanted fat. If you happen to have a scale lying around in your house somewhere, then don't be afraid of using it. Doing so could actually help you keep unwanted pounds off while you train.

Bring a chart with you to the gym so that you can write your progress down. Every 14 days, weigh yourself, and have a personal trainer, or anybody that is experienced, check your body fat. Be patient and take your time. Things aren't just going to happen overnight. Keep in mind that in order to achieve these goals, you will need to follow a healthy, strict diet. After all, hard work and dedication is the only way to go.

Chapter 4

Ultimate Fat Burning Strategies

Most people may think that in order to burn fat, all it takes is to just eat a small salad, and go do some cardio. The funny thing about it is that you won't see much in the way of results doing it that way.

Fat burning is a process. For some, the fat burning process could take longer than others, depending on what their fat percentages is. However, for most the strategies of train safely, eat healthy, and get plenty of rest will do wonders.

Strength Train Safely

Failure to work out safely could result in you getting injured. Once you become injured, guess what happens? You have to stop training to give your injury time to heal. The bad news is, while you are healing, the fat storage you were trying to get rid of will start to add up. The best way to avoid anything bad from happening is to not train with too heavy of weights.

Heavy weight training will make you train with sloppy form. Leave that for the power lifters, pro body builders, or those who are training for the strong man competition. Most people forget the meaning of training is actually exercise, which is for being in shape and healthy.

Oftentimes, their conception is to get as big as possible so that they can walk around with their arms spread out giving most the impression that they used bad deodorant. Being big is not always better. Sorry, I am not trying to discredit the big guys, but this is something you should keep in mind. If you can't get your back to grow for that cobra like appearance, no need to fake it. Chances are, you might not be training your back properly.

I am also not saying it is okay to look boney, either. What I am saying is that there is a right way to do things.

Try to avoid overtraining, which is another common mistake that can cause injury. Overtraining can also lead to fatigue, and it can even slow down the metabolism.

Keep Your Cardio Creative

Another secret weapon that is good for fat burning is cardio. Not a lot of people enjoy doing cardio, because, to them, it is either boring or just plain tiring. There are many different varieties of exercises that can help to keep things fresh, such as cycling, jump roping, running, walking, or even water aerobic—which could definitely be beneficial to those with knee, back, or joint problems.

Keep in mind that cardio can also be done by using many different cardio machines.

The goal when doing cardio is to bring your inner body temperature high so that you are at the rate for cutting down the unwanted body fat.

Start by using the treadmill. The required time should be 45 minutes, three to five times a week. Remember, you don't always have to run. Start off at a moderate walking pace, gradually bringing the speed up every five to ten minutes until you begin to build a sweat. You will soon be seeing the unwanted fat melt off like butter.

You will also start to feel good about doing cardio. Part of this is due to the natural endorphins the body releases, which makes a person feel so good after exercising. Overtime, you will begin to appreciate cardio much more.

LESSEN YOUR CARB INTAKE

Besides, in addition to doing cardio, you might want to take it easy with the carbohydrates. Too many carbohydrates are very bad for the body, especially if you are only consuming processed or white carbohydrates, such as a lot of potatoes, white bread, white pasta, and white rice.

This doesn't mean that you should ditch your carbohydrates. Without any, your brain cannot function right. This is basically fuel it uses in order to keep going properly. It's also something that the body requires for making energy. The best way you can prevent yourself from loading up on the wrong carbohydrates are to choose the right ones that the body requires for good health and functioning.

For example fresh vegetables, whole wheat pasta, whole grain breads, and brown rice are excellent sources of good carbohydrates. This means you should be consuming carbohydrates that contain low glycemic index. This ensures a lower delivery for insulin, which, in turn, promotes healthy blood glucose, which reduces the levels of blood lipids, otherwise known as fats.

Along with watching and carefully planning a lean diet that includes whole grain carbohydrates, try throwing in a natural fat burner or supplement, preferably a type that doesn't have much ephedrine in it. If you have a heart problem, then I highly suggest that you speak to your doctor before touching any fat burner. These natural fat burners include coconut oil, chromium picolinate, choline, glucomannan, mahaung, coq10, 5htp, olive oil, mct's, cla's, protein, yohimbine, chirosan, letchin, and l-carnitine.

Follow a Strict Diet Regimen

Aside from doing cardio and taking fat burners, you must also remember to add a strict diet regimen to your plan as well. Again the plan here is to add lean muscle in order to melt that fat off. In this day and age, a lean physique can be really attractive to the ladies and might even bring you closer to one when you're least expecting it.

Lean muscle is also better to have for burning calories. Even as you rest muscles can amp up your metabolism. An excellent way to do this is by doing resistance training.

Hydrate Regularly

When training hard and you want to burn fat, you have to add water to your diet as well. You should, at least, be drinking a gallon to two a day. It is the key to giving life and also for burning fat. In addition, water keeps you hydrated as you train.

This liquid is all natural. Although there are also bottled water that comes in flavored varieties, stay away from that stuff. Yes, some do contain added nutrients and preservatives, but regular water is better. Stick to it instead. It will better help to flush out your system and also process the appetite, which also increases your metabolic rate. So drink up!

Eat Fewer, Smaller Meals

Believe it or not, when you are trying to get rid of fat, starving yourself is definitely not the way to go. Other people might think that since they are trying to get rid of their excess weight, this is the key to succeed. The first and best way to succeed in fighting off unwanted fat is to eat at least five to six or small meals, rather than consuming three big meals, a day.

Sometimes, depending on your body type, adding one more meal to your diet plan can't hurt you, nor will it get you fat. Eating five, six, or seven small meals a day is what it will take to ensure that you are burning what you are trying to burn off and get rid of for good. Because it quickens the metabolism, the more small meals you feed the body, the better it is for you as long as you are adding plenty of exercise in your plan, also.

There is a catch to this mechanism. The goal is to consume healthy, nutritious food, not junk. Avoid eating three big meals; this will only slow your metabolism down and give your body a chance to let the fat collect, especially in your love handles or areas that you don't want it the most.

Eat More Natural Fat Burning Foods

One of the ways to implement healthier cooking alternatives is to adopt a low-fat diet or style of eating, especially if you want to live a healthier life and want to live longer.

In addition to helping you burn fat, eating healthy also builds up your immune system. It is also vital that you pay attention to the foods that you are putting into your body. A low-fat diet is also one of the popular ways to stay healthy.

Cooking low-fat recipes and being conscious of your health is the way you want to be. After all, although high-fat foods may taste good at the moment, just imagine what your body and health will be like in the future.

However, there is good news! The good news is that there are natural foods out there that can actually help you burn fat and that considered to be natural fat burners. Amazingly, they are not difficult to find.

NEGATIVE CALORIE FOODS

These foods are known as negative calorie foods. This means that there are foods that require more energy to burn then they provide. Some of these foods are celery, spinach, and apples.

CITRUS FRUITS

There is another group of natural foods that are not fat burners. The good news is citrus fruits may not be negative calorie food burners, but they do perform a helpful function in weight loss programs. Citrus fruits help your body get rid of fats. It also helps your body to process fats more efficiently and quickly.

Coconut Products

Coconut oil and coconuts are also considered to be another natural fat burner. This natural food is very helpful in many ways. It was also used by the women of India to treat hair, skin, and weight problems. Fat burning natural foods are not hard to find. You can find them at your local supermarket.

Root Vegetables

If you are trying to lose weight, then try root vegetables. Root vegetables are packed with fiber and are very nutritious. Root vegetables are carrots, radishes, rutabagas, parsnips, and turnips. Don't be afraid to throw in some scallions, chives, leaks, shallots, and onions, too! These are very tasty and can be added to any dish.

These foods may seem boring and not much fun to eat, but they sure can help you burn fat. By eating these natural products, you will not only burn fat effortlessly, you will also feel better too.

Get Enough Sleep

Exercising and eating right are vital for fat burning, but so is getting a sufficient amount of rest. I'm sure you might have heard this before, but the ideal amount of rest is 8 to 10 hours. It is said that those who get at least 8 or 10 hours of rest are usually much leaner than people who are not meeting their standards. Also, when a person gets plenty of rest, their leptin levels are much higher, giving them a much faster metabolism for burning fat, versus a person who gets six hours of rest. The fewer hours you sleep you receive, the less leptin levels you have.

Leptins, are based on how much fat your body has, which is what causes a person's appetite to be lost. People who suffer from obesity are usually the ones with less leptin and what it does to the appetite.

So, again, the less sleep you get, the less leptin you have, which then causes extreme hunger, which could then lead to over eating, especially the wrong foods.

Chapter 5

Sleep and Starting Your Day the Right Way

Briefly mentioned in the previous chapter, in order to get the energy that you need and to have your body to respond well to your training, you have to get the right amount of sleep. Without it, you simply can't focus well, and you also won't be able to train at 100%.

Not getting enough rest leads to stress, fatigue, headaches, and also brings up your aggression level. The body needs at least 8 to 10 hours of rest. Unfortunately, there are a good amount of people who fail to get even 6 hours of rest. The reason for this is because some of them maybe working long hours or could be in school, and they get so carried away with working or studying that they don't make that time for themselves to get the right amount of sleep that they need.

Getting rest is as important as proper nutrition, and it also keeps you happy, healthy, and looking young.

Sleep for Energy

Just like the importance of eating healthy, sleep is another important factor. 8-10 hours of it is just what we all need for good health reasons.

Believe me when I say this, if you set yourself up for the challenge of eating for energy and get plenty of sleep every night, you will definitely notice how low your stress and fatigue levels will become. Your mood and tolerance with other people around will improve as well as your alertness.

Remember, your energy levels are at their highest in the mornings before dropping as the day progresses. The only true way to obtain and maintain high energy is to get an adequate amount of rest at night. As your circadian rhythms improve, you will begin to feel results and get healthier.

I always make sure that I go to bed early so that when I wake up in the morning, my brain is charged and my body is energized.

Supplements for Sleep Aid

If you are not sleeping well at night and don't want to take any sleeping aids for fear of building dependency, then fear no more. Here are three natural supplements that will have you sleeping in a matter of minutes and keep you in bed for as long as 9 hours. These three supplements also help raise the levels of anabolic hormones, growth hormones, known as (GH), and testosterone.

Phenibut 4-amino-3-phenylbutanoic acid, phenibut gab is also known as phenibut. It is a neurotransmitter that helps the body stay calm and get rest by inhibiting stimulatory neurotransmitters. It also helps boost go levels.

Phenibut is connected to the same receptor that gab does to cause the same effect. It increases the body's own production of GABA, which is sometimes called phgaba. The recommended dosage for phenibut is 100-300 mg on an empty stomach, preferably 30 minutes before bedtime.

TRYPTOPHAN

5-HTP or 5-Hydroxy-Tryptophan, also known as Tryptophan is a modified version of an amino acid. It forms serotonin and melatonin neurotransmitters and hormones that help you relax and sleep better.

It also boosts levels of gone detrain, releasing luteinizing hormones in men, which can also lead to more testosterone production. Recommended dosage should be 50 to 300 mg on an empty stomach, 30 minutes before bed.

Thiamine This amino acid is responsible for providing the calming effect of green tea. Thiamine may also help improve sleep quality and relaxation. Thiamine also promotes brain alpha—and wave function. The recommended dosage should be 200-500 mg on an empty stomach, preferably 30 minutes before bed.

THE DANGERS OF USING CAFFEINE

If you're having difficulty sleeping, before taking supplements to help, perhaps first take a look at your caffeine intake. Caffeine can play a huge role in your ability to sleep at night, wake up in the morning, and have consistent energy levels throughout the day.

Many who have a difficult time waking up in the morning (often due to simply an insufficient amount of sleep), often look for ways to get the body's energy in what they think is a quick fix (coffee, energy drink, soda, etc.) simply to get through the day. However, there are certain effects that caffeine can have on the body that are making your energy levels worse, not better.

These days, there are many varieties of caffeinated drinks and products to choose from, such as coffee, energy drinks, and sodas. The bad part is that not a lot of them list the amount of caffeine these drinks contain. Some energy drinks can contain the same amount of caffeine as at least 10 to 12 cans Coca-Cola, which can give you an edge that can basically take you out of your mind, giving you quick burst of energy. However, just as rapidly as it gives you an energy burst, it will bring you crashing down to a halt.

Excessive caffeine can also intoxicate you. There are health risks with caffeine, which means you should always be careful of the amounts of energy drinks that you consume. When a person is intoxicated from large amounts of caffeine that they take in, it really makes them jittery, nervous, sleepless, anxious, experience gastrointestinal upset, rapid heart beating, and insomnia.

Energy drinks even contain more caffeine than soda or coffee. Coffee actually contains antioxidants, such as chlorosenic acid and melanoidins. Antioxidants in the coffee helps to play a role in preventing oxidation, which is a process that leads to damage in the cells and aging and reduces the risk of developing Parkinson disease, Type-2 diabetes, liver cirrhosis, alcoholic cirrhosis, gallstones, kidney stones, Alzheimer's disease, improves asthma, and improves mental performance.

Although coffee has its good side, it also can cause negativity in health as well. Excessive caffeine can lead to risks of coronary heart disease, high cholesterol, the functioning of the blood vessel tone, rapid heartbeat, hypertension, osteoporosis, heartburn, upsetting the sleep-cycle, dehydration, and caffeine addiction. This shows you that no matter how tired you feel in the morning or during the day, you should always choose your caffeine intake wisely.

STARTING YOUR DAY THE RIGHT WAY

I like to begin my day with a good breakfast that is high in protein and a right amount of carbohydrates. Some people don't even do breakfast at all and sometimes wait until much later to have lunch, which, at times, happens to end up being energy-less food that is consumed, such as something either really sweet, chips, and/or a soda,

Though you do not have to eat breakfast as soon as you wake up, it still isn't a good idea to skip it, because it sure helps after a good night's rest to rev up your energy levels for whatever day that lies ahead.

I tend to have my breakfast at least three hours after I wake up so that I have food into my system by the time I get to work, and I have not starved myself before lunch. The reason that I don't want to starve myself before I have lunch is because I don't want to overeat when lunch time rolls around.

Occasionally, I may wake up even earlier than the usual time I get up, but I still have my breakfast at the same time and pack myself a midmorning snack to munch on while I am at work for when hunger strikes.

When a person is hungry, it is extremely difficult to perform daily tasks, and this can sometimes get you behind on your work. Types of snacks that I like to bring in can range from yogurt, fruit, low-fat wheat thins, and natural unsalted almonds mixed with raisins and yogurt bits.

Sometimes, I may just keep it plain and simple by sticking to only unsalted almonds by themselves. I find that snacking helps me avoid calorie overloading during lunch time, and it also helps with fatigue.

Try to go for low calorie morning snacks, because they are what will take the pressure of hunger off you while you are busy, enabling you to function at 100%.

There are many mouth-watering food choices to choose from. Between all the foods that are available, the choice can be very tricky sometimes, causing confusion and leading one to choose the wrong food.

Breakfasts that you have in the morning may be high in both carbohydrates and fiber, but they can sometimes lack vitamins and minerals, due to wrong choices of foods. It's a common mistake that most make before they actually find out what foods are really good for the body.

It is important that you choose your breakfast wisely, preferably ones that are rich in these minerals, and choose ones that provide you with energy to handle all of your daily tasks.

LEARN TO MAKE WISE BREAKFAST CHOICES AT HOME

We all hold different types of jobs, where some of us are required to leave home to go to work, while others get to work out of the comfort of their own homes. Working from home can have its benefits and its consequences as well.

If you were to work from home, you should always try to take the time to sit down and have a nutritious breakfast. Let's look at the great advantage of working from your home. For example, the best thing about that is the fact that everything is right there beside you, and therefore, you do not need to travel as far to get what you need.

Another thing is that you don't have to worry about spending money so much every morning. Simply just have a stock of all the healthy foods that you need ready for cooking. By having a good amount of healthy food stocked and ready for consumption, you will not have to make the mistake of counting yourself out from getting the proper nutrients that you need for building optimum energy.

You should know how to treat yourself as well as you would normally do for your spouse and kids. Say, if you were working from your home, you would have to take the advantage of eating proper nutrients in the morning.

Another thing is try to set yourself up with a schedule to eat on a normal basis of every 2 to 3 hours. If you are not hungry, have a light snack in between meals so that hunger does not sneak up on you, and you can continue having energy to get your job done. Never skip meals, because you do not want to end up overeating at the next one.

Due to the fact that you may be working from home, overeating would be the last thing you would want to do, mainly because it can lead you to feeling really sluggish and sleepy. This can lead you to want to take a nap when you should be working. Overeating is a way of setting yourself up for many other things, including weight gain. Weight gain can also come from eating at all odd hours and becoming careless about what you eat.

Skipping breakfast is never a great thing to do, which is something that can be all too common among many Americans. Besides, skipping breakfast will make you pretty hungry later during the day, and you know what that means: you will listen to your appetite and eat whatever you want without thinking twice. Over time, you will suffer the consequences, which can lead to weight gain later.

If you dedicate about 10 to 15 minutes of breakfast time every morning, it may, in fact, help you to cut calories and lose unwanted, extra weight, where you least want it.

However, this can only happen if you are eating the right foods. Before you know it, you will be well, energetic, feel much better throughout the day, work more effectively, and also be more successful at the work that you do in the comfort of your home.

MAKING TIME FOR BREAKFAST

When a person has a really busy schedule that they have to deal with everyday, things can get pretty hectic, which can also put a strain on your health and other parts of your personal life. Often times, a busy schedule may cause you to skip out on one of the most important things that you should always do after waking up: eating breakfast. Although some of us tend to have a much busier more demanding schedule than others, taking that special time out to eat and enjoy breakfast can help you relieve some stress off of your busy day that you have waiting ahead of you.

Beginning the day by having breakfast can make a difference on how you will perform your daily tasks. Skipping breakfast can cause your functioning levels to fail, which can also take a toll on your body's health over time. Needless to say, your health comes first. Of course, many people realize this, but they fail to practice what they preach.

In fact, some people completely cut out breakfast as their first morning priority, because they are never really hungry in the mornings and don't feel the need for it. Others simply feel that taking the time to sit down at home to have breakfast is a waste of time.

LEARNING TO LOVE BREAKFAST: A TRUE STORY

I have met people who go by this believe, and one of them happens to be a good long time friend of mine. We both work at the same job together. Besides work, he is also a musician, who has his own music group, which he is always rehearsing with every day, also on the weekends. He also frequently travels and even stays up late every night to work on his music. He is a really busy guy.

However, when he wakes up the next day to come to work, he is like a zombie. Because of the lifestyle my buddy lives, I can see why he is always so tired every morning. First of all, he does not eat breakfast at home, which causes him to always be hungry a few hours after arriving at work. Why? Well, he never really tries to put in the time to take care of his nutritional needs after waking up. You see, we both take fifteen minute breaks at the same time, which normally isn't until about ten thirty or so by then. At that time, he is really hungry. When he finally gets the time to get some breakfast into his system, his food choices are really poor. He tends to go after the really sweet things and, not to mention, adds an energy drink to top it off. By the time he has had his fill, the complaints of belly aches and headaches begin.

One thing I have noticed about him is once he has had breakfast, his energy levels are high. However, after a while, he crashes back down to where he first started at when he first came into work in the morning.

After watching him go through this cycle for weeks, I decided to pull him aside and share with him some of my health tips and what I could do to help him. I also told him that if he kept up with this act of not having a well-balanced, nutritious breakfast every morning before beginning his day, it would affect his job, music, and his health in the long run. He took my advice and followed through with taking the time to eat breakfast every day. Not only that, but he also chose to eat the right foods.

What I did was write down a simple breakfast food chart of all the right foods that contained great nutrients, such as vitamins, minerals, proteins, and carbohydrates. I even went on to write foods that made good mid-morning snacks to eat, foods for lunch, and good foods that he could use as dinner at home while he was cooking for his fiancée. Additionally, he also learned to pre-pack his meals the night before, so that way, he didn't have to worry about rushing and not having time to eat breakfast or pack his food.

He even cut out the late night rehearsals as well to get more hours of sleep, which was something I also told him to do if he ever wanted to not be so tired in the mornings.

Once my friend began following the breakfast chart, my eating tips, and getting more sleep, he was a new person. No sooner than a few days had passed and I began noticing a really big difference in his performance at work.

When I asked him about how he was doing nutrition-wise, he told me everything was going great. He thanked me and told me that he had never in his life felt better. He was determined to continue eating for energy, because after only a few days, he could already begin to see what an amazing transformation choosing the right foods at the right times was going to have in his life.

WHY BREAKFAST IS THE KEY TO ALL DAY ENERGY

When waking up in the morning, the body's blood sugar or glucose levels are very low. This occurs after a person has been asleep for 7-10 hours, which normally causes the body to want to be fed. You have to remember first things first. The number one thing to do after waking up is to always start the day off with a big, healthy breakfast. Most people fail to do his. This is the reason why it is called breakfast, which means to break the fast. By breaking the fast, you are actually replenishing the body's needs for glucose and providing it as energy for the body's use. Not only does breakfast provides energy for the body, but it also provides energy for the brain. This is important, because the brain needs the glucose to feed on.

Eating breakfast in the morning also helps you concentrate better, making you sharper in the morning and making you ready to take on any task or other activity that might await you at work or throughout the day. This may even make you less angry and irritable when dealing with other people.

Glucose is also important because it feeds the muscles, so you will feel more energized and less tired. Not only is it crucial that you eat a nutritious breakfast, but it's also best to make it a big one. Avoid products that are high in sugars. Sure, it will give you energy, but only for a short period of time. Then it will bring your body down, giving you a sugar crash, making you even hungrier. This is also bad, because it may lead to excess weight gain.

Eating a breakfast that is both high in nutrients and loaded with whole grains is considered to be a smarter choice. Whole grains digest better and provide the best for your body over the fatty, sweet junk food that's out there. And I love being able to say that this also gives you energy throughout the day.

Sugary Cereals: Yes or No?

By whole grains, do I mean sweet sugary "whole grain" kiddie cereal? No! It is always best to stay clear of sweet, sugary cereals only because of the effects of what a lot of sugar may do to.

Remember, your goal in the morning is to eat a healthy breakfast that will give you long lasting energy, not short term energy. Try cereals such as Fiber One or All Bran cereal. As funny as this may sound, these types of cereals can even be eaten for lunch, which is also good for helping you lose weight. For example, if you were to consume a daily total of 640 fewer calories, you would lose about 2-4 pounds in a two to three week time period.

The best thing about it is that although the original brand may be pricey, there is also an alternative store brand. This type of food is also an easy to use food, which works better with low-fat milk.

Why Not to Skip Breakfast

Energy is one of the keys to happiness and health. Keep in mind that skipping breakfast will lead to weight gain and eating breakfast will do the opposite. Consider it bad verses good. It is always best to fit this important regimen into your schedule before walking out that door. If you are a person with a tight schedule, then try pre-packing your breakfast and even lunch so that they are ready for you in the morning. Start off with something small, such as a piece of wheat bread toast with a little bit of fat-free butter or peanut butter, and then slowly work your way up to a bigger and healthier breakfast as your body gets accustomed to having it.

Not only does the body get the proper nutrients and energy that it needs in the morning, this also leaves you satisfied and full, preventing you from buying junk food on the go.

By doing this, you are doing yourself a favor both in the gut department and also in the pocket department, saving you lots of money for, who knows, maybe that nice watch that you've always had your eye on or whatever comes your way.

Besides saving money and your health, you will be less hungry during lunch time. This also works out because eating small amounts of food during your lunch break allows you to eat very little by late evening until bed time. This is the first step to what it takes for getting you to achieving a flat stomach. Think of this process as the domino effect.

Healthy Breakfast Foods Revealed

All this talk of what to eat/what not to eat may have your mind spinning right about now. So, let me introduce a few examples of some of my favorite healthy breakfast foods to help you out.

Egg Whites

These are low in fat, high in protein, and also go really well with a bowl of oatmeal. They can be made into a breakfast sandwich with two slices of toasted wheat bread or your choice of a few, thin slices of lean turkey bacon and a whole wheat English muffin.

PLAIN OATMEAL

Plain oatmeal contains a good source of high fiber, which is also excellent for controlling cholesterol, digests slowly in the body, and is a good energy booster. It is also a complex carbohydrate. Plain oatmeal is also better than instant oatmeal, because it doesn't contain unnecessary sugars.

BEANS

Beans are high in fiber and help reduce the risk of developing cancers and heart disease. There are also plenty of other types of beans to choose from. They are high in antioxidants, which help to neutralize the free radicals in the body. Not only are they delicious, but they also can be fixed with any meal.

QUINOA

This seed makes a perfect substitute for brown rice. It is also light and can be eaten as a warm breakfast cereal, added to salads, and also comes in a variation of colors. These include yellow, white, red, and black. Quinoa seed also comes in a form of flakes as well. Quinoa also helps to treat certain symptoms, such as acute chronic inflammatory disease. It also helps to improve your mood.

Fish

Fish is a great source of lean protein, and it is high in poly saturated Omega-3 fatty acids, such as docosaneyaenoic acid, which is DHA, and eicosapentaenoic acid, which is EPA. These fatty acids help reduce the risk of developing coronary heart disease and may also improve circulation by preventing blood clots and reducing blood pressure. There other types of fish that you can also use to improve your health as well these include: salmon, tuna, and mackerel.

Nuts

Unsalted, dried nuts contain high antioxidants and healthy fats. They are also high in minerals, which help to reduce the risk of developing cardiovascular disease, Alzheimer's disease, Type-2 diabetes, and even certain types of cancers. Nuts can also help play a role in cutting fat and preventing you to gain unwanted excess weight. These are considered to be a dense food, which also has high levels of vitamins, minerals, micronutrients and is a good source of fiber, protein, and energy for the body and brain. The reason why nuts can make a perfect snack is because they can keep you nice and full. However, not all types of nuts contain the same amounts of antioxidants.

The best way to enjoy them is to have them unsalted. They are also good to eat with salads, granola, oatmeal, and yogurt.

CRUCIFEROUS VEGETABLES

These include cabbage, broccoli, cauliflower, Brussels sprouts, kale, and radishes. These are all considered to be cruciferous type vegetables, because they all contain Vitamin C soluble fiber and nutrients that have anticancer properties. These anticancer properties are able to fight off certain cancers and also contain diindolyimethane, which is a type of compound of sulforaphane and selenium. These vegetables also help to suppress the cell proliferation in prostate cancer cells.

They can be eaten raw, stir-fried with beef or any meat, or cooked in any other creative way of your choosing. It is best to cook these foods with light olive oil.

APPLES

Apples are a healthy fruit that are high in fiber and contain fruit pectin, soluble fiber, a high amount of antioxidants, vitamins, and trace minerals. Apples also help to reduce the risk of developing colon cancer, prostate cancer, and lung cancer. They also contain a good source of quercetin, epicatechin, procyanidin, and Vitamin B2. They are low in calories. They do not contain any cholesterol and are a fat-free food. Additionally, apples can also be added to oatmeal, cold cereals, salads, or can eaten by themselves.

BERRIES

These include raspberries, blackberries, blueberries, cranberries, and strawberries. All the berries that I have just mentioned above all are good sources of antioxidants and are low in fat. They contain sources of fiber and are low in sugar and low carbohydrates. They can also be enjoyed with a nice sized bowl of oatmeal in the morning or even a smoothie.

GREEN LEAFY VEGETABLES

Green leafy vegetables are low in calories and are a good source of antioxidants, vitamins, and minerals. The good thing about them is that they can be eaten as a side salad along with any meal. The best dressings to use on them are a vinaigrette, low-fat dressing, so that way, you are not getting robbed of vitamins and minerals. Leafy green vegetables also help to promote fat burning.

Other good vegetables that are good to use are kale, spinach, and basically all dark, leafy-type vegetables.

ORANGE JUICE

A glass of orange juice a day is one of the best choices to have with any healthy breakfast. It can be enjoyed any time during the day, and it is good to fight off colds or even help to prevent one. This potent liquid is a good source of antioxidants and Vitamin C. It may also help to reduce the risk of developing cardiovascular disease and improve blood pressure. Orange juice can help to improve healthy cells that line the blood vessels by providing a good source of potassium and containing about 292 milligrams of hesporidina.

This is a juice that can go well with a bowl of cold cereal.

BANANAS

This fruit is a good source of potassium and contains roughly about 467-mg and 1-mg of sodium. Bananas help to maintain good blood pressure and are good for the functioning of the heart, protecting against artherosclerosis, and reduces the chance of developing future strokes when combined with foods that are high in magnesium and fiber. Not to mention, bananas also helps to reduce the risk of developing chronic heart disease, diabetes, and stomach ulcers. Bananas are good for replenishing the potassium in the body and regulating fluid balance as well.

This fruit contains pectin, which can normalize the digestive tract. Bananas also protects eyesight. Bananas also helps to improve calcium absorption, promotes healthy kidneys, and are rich in fructooligosqccharide, Vitamin C, magnesium, and fiber.

This fruit can be eaten with cereal, a smoothie, yogurt, and fruit salad. The suggested amount should at least be 3 or more per day.

Keep in mind that this small list was just an example of the healthy breakfast foods that can be chosen and can also be mixed with any other healthy foods to ensure that you are getting the proper amount of vitamins and minerals that your body needs. The next chapter discusses additional, healthy foods for optimal energy.

CHAPTER 6

THE RIGHT FOOD CHOICES FOR ENERGY

Have you ever experienced one of those days when you just didn't feel like going to the gym or didn't feel like doing anything at all, because you might have felt extremely tired after an eight hour shift? Well, don't feel bad. Sometimes, it just means that the body needs a little rest, because it has been pushed too hard.

Some people may think of themselves as machines and unstoppable, but believe me, we are all humans. Moments like these happens to all of us, even athletes. This is when foods that are high in energy are very important. These foods are crucial to ensure that we get enough energy to complete the day or get us through whatever needs to get done, especially in preparation for a workout.

When choosing these foods, it is important that they are eaten in a carefully balanced way. You should also eat a good mixture of carbohydrates, which include vegetables, potatoes, fruits, berries and whole grains, and proteins, such as red and white meats, eggs, fish, and nuts.

It is important to watch how you take in your carbohydrates. The body can only burn so much fat at a time. This is something you must be able to balance. If you are not eating enough carbohydrates, you won't be able to get enough energy. However, if you eat too much of it, there is a possibility that you may end up packing on unwanted weight.

CARBOHYDRATES FOR ENERGY

It is important that you eat the right kinds of carbohydrates. For example, eating carbohydrates that are high in sugar will only give you short energy boosts, which can be good for short periods. However, for the long run, they can make you gain weight.

To avoid experiencing up and down energy levels, it would be best to not starve yourself in between meals, because doing so will affect your blood sugar, which is the factor behind your up and down energy levels. In order to reach a high energy mark, you should be eating healthy snacks every two to three hours.

Whole grains, such as bread, cereal, rice, and pasta are important sources of carbohydrates, and they also make up the basis of your diet. It is best to try to eat between six to eleven servings a day.

Keep in mind that it is important to distinguish between whole and refined grains and to also make the right choice of choosing whole grains. There are certain starchy foods that may have a negative affection on health. For example, if your diet were to consist primarily of potatoes, white rice, and other foods made from refined white or enriched wheat flour, you would have a higher risk of developing diabetes and cardiovascular disease than those who eat primarily from whole grains.

Try to get your carbohydrates from whole grain foods, such as whole wheat bread, brown rice, and whole wheat pasta. Try to limit the amount of refined products.

By including whole grains in your diet, you may lower the risk of cardiovascular disease. The reason for this is because whole grains are low in saturated fat and high in fiber, vitamins, minerals, and antioxidants. Whole grains are also an important source of protein when combined with legumes or dairy products.

Grains can also be eaten processed or whole and mixed into hot or cold cereals or flour from many different food products, such as breads muffins, and soups. Grains are a perfect source or vitamins and minerals, especially b vitamins, calcium, potassium, and phosphorus.

Healthy grains that are good to use include whole wheat, oats, corn, barley, millet, quinoa, rye, wild rice, and brown rice.

HYDRATION FOR ENERGY

It is also important that your body stays fully hydrated. Being hydrated is very crucial as it will not allow you to be fatigued as much and will also give the muscles the water that they need. Drinking plenty of water is good for helping to flush out those nasty toxins, which can prevent you from getting a good amount of energy. This would also mean that anyone who tends to make unhealthy choices would have to cut back on the alcohol consumption and excessive caffeine, such as coffee, sugary energy drinks, or energy shots. Also, if you tend to use a lot of salt in your food, now would be the best time to cut back. Too much of it will make you retain a lot of water and make you look and feel bloated and sluggish.

Replenishing fluids can also help to keep you full, especially water. In fact, water makes a much healthier choice than all other drinks that are available for all consumers.

There are also other drinks that are available if you find water to be a very boring beverage. Another option may include fruit juices, but be very careful that the fruit juice that you choose does not contain too much sugar, which is very common amongst juices that are sold out of regular grocery stores. Instead choose something that contains at least 100% fruit juice and is not from concentrate. That way, you are getting a good amount of extra vitamins on the side.

Avoid beverages like soda and alcohol. If you cannot completely stay away from either of these two, at least try to have these in very small moderations or only once in a while. Not only are these two types of drinks unhealthy for you, too much of either can cause a serious health risks. This is especially in regards to alcohol, which can cause the effects of making you do things like slowing you down and leading you to forget to eat the right foods at the right time.

CHAPTER 7

THE RIGHT TIME FOR ENERGY

WHAT IS ENERGY?

We are all familiar with the word energy. The question is, do you know what energy is made up of, and how food becomes energy for your body? You are about to find out.

First off, many of us may recognize energy as a presence or potential that allows things to be performed. For example, light is made up of energy. This includes other sources, such as electric energy, chemical, heat, and mechanical. Let's put it this way: if there was no such thing as energy, then there simply wouldn't be any life or even a universe.

Energy is the main reason why life is what it is today. Energy is a source that can turn one form into another, which also goes to say that energy in the universe is always constant. Different forms of it can always change from one to another. So, in reality, energy is something that can't be made up or destroyed.

If you were to look at your ceiling or the lamp in your room after turning the switch on, it would obviously light up. The reason why the bulb would light up is because it contains a very thin filament inside it. What makes the light appear is the electric energy that is coming from the wall socket, which is then converted through the cord to the little thin filament in the bulb, turning the energy into two types of forms: heat and light. When the filament is illuminating, the electrical energy reduces, causing the energy from the heat and light to increase. In that case, the energy gets converted to other forms and also can never get lost.

Now, let's get back to nutrition. All food that we eat contains at least some form of chemical energy. These chemical energies may come from fats, carbohydrates, alcohol, and proteins. As soon as the food is consumed the chemical energy that comes from it, turns into mechanical energy and is used or fuel to help power up muscular movement, body heat, and normal daily activities. When we do not use these energy molecules immediately, our bodies end up storing them for much later use. Although we acquire energy from foods in form of proteins, fats, carbohydrates, and alcohol, we just cannot use the molecules directly, because our bodies were not meant to function that way.

The substances that we consume must first go through a chemical reaction pathway phase that allows them to be broken down, enabling us to get the energy in the proper form, from which we then can use directly. Food energy is also stored in our bodies for later use when it's really needed. Let's break this down a little. For example, whenever the energy molecules are broken down, a little of that energy is captured in a source called high energy molecules. To make things more understandable, when our bodies need energy for power, it uses special molecules that helps to boost the body for activities, such as sports and other movements that require the use of energy. Once the body receives the energy that it needs, it uses the source with a controlled manner. Not to mention, there are specific enzymes that are set to team up with these special molecules with an energy-requiring, chemical reaction and the use of energy.

True is the fact that energy is released in the breaking down of proteins, fats, carbohydrates, and alcohol. This does not mean that all of it gets incorporated into the special molecules known as (A.T.P) Adenosine Triphosphate. Our bodies are at least able to obtain somewhere between 43 to 45 percent of energy, which is always available in the molecule formation of A.T.P. Whatever is left behind, which may sometimes be around 54 to 60 percent, is turned into energy for the body to use as heat for the regulation of body temperature.

CIRCADIAN RHYTHMS: ENERGY UPS AND DOWNS

Let's move onto a subject that most people have already heard of and are, therefore, familiar with: (regular and predictable biological ups and downs, also known as circadian rhythms.

The body experiences this mentally and physically when it comes to energy levels, repeating this cycle every twenty four hours.

I am going to share with you an idea of how to use food for brain power and how food has an effect on the brain's chemistry, helping us to make our biological cycle better when it is going through tough times. What I'm really going to do is guide you to the right foods for keeping your mental energy levels at their peak, even when predictable biological ups and downs threaten to bring them at a low point.

Every living organism on this planet experiences this, so this is normal. Don't feel bad. Our bodies act like internal clocks by making us feel energetic as soon as we wake up, right? Let a little time go by, and before you know it, energy levels start to slump, causing the brain to have less power. Therefore, this stops the brain from functioning properly.

Do you remember when I mentioned earlier in the book on how we were all built differently? We all have different levels of down energy that we go through, which means that some of us experience more fatigue than others or just don't have the same amounts of energy to begin with. One thing that we may all share in common is the fact that our energy levels tend to drop before bedtime, no matter what time it is that you happen to be hitting the sack. This is normal. However, if it is at a low, when it's supposed to be at a high, that would not be considered to be normal. No matter what type of person or energy level a person has, it seems that one's mental energy and high alertness is at its highest, roughly, around five hours after awakening. After those five hours have passed, the body slowly starts to wear down as you get tired, causing grogginess and sometimes grumpiness until we finally get that chance to fix the situation with sleep. Again.

There are times when the body can be extremely tired on certain days even before the lunch hour. Sometimes, this is known to happen even if you might have gotten a really good night's rest the night before. In addition, one's energy levels can also vary depending on the amount of food that you eat and, most importantly, what type of it you consume.

The behavioral process of the (human biological clock) circadian rhythms is really powerful. In fact, this is exactly what helps to keep your cells on track by sending messages to the glands and letting them know when the right time is to either increase or decrease the production of certain kinds of hormones and also regulating the volumes of energy and body temperature. Keep in mind that this is what makes you feel the way you do whenever you perform in any kind of energy related activity. In order to ensure that you obtain the right kind of energy and enough of it for the day, you have to be willing and dedicated to planning on changing your normal diet if it isn't already energy giving.

Eating the Right Foods at the Right Time

Eating energy rich foods can help you achieve more and do your best at whatever you do, regardless of whether it is at school, the gym, personal life, or at work. One important factor that you shouldn't forget is eating the right food at the right time. Additionally, you also have to be sure that this falls perfectly well with your biological clock. You should always consume foods that interact with your biological clock, because it will help you maintain high levels of energy, even during times when you would normally be tired during the day.

May I tell you, during the beginning of your transformation to eating for energy, it is actually going to take some getting used to for your body; not for it to feel the difference by having more energy, but more less in the sense of how serious and how far you are willing to go to make that switch from low energy foods to high energy foods. When you finally have committed yourself to doing this, you will be in a better mood, and you will definitely feel the difference in the new you.

Believe me, it is not as hard as you think it is. Once you get your internal clock used to these foods, successfully, you're golden. Although food can help influence your brain's production of alertness chemicals, such as norepinephrine, serotonin, which helps to calm you, and dopamine, certain foods have more of these effects on the brain than others. This gives you a longer-lasting supply of energy and helps you have control of your high energy and low energy levels that affect your performance and the way that you feel.

The Importance of Power Eating

It's worth it to eat for energy, or, should I say, "power eat" your way for good energy. Power eating is something that can energize the mind, mood, and alertness for the positive things, while maximizing the brain and energy when they are at peak.

One really good advise that I am giving you is power eat throughout the day, starting from breakfast, to lunch, to snack, and dinner. The point of power eating is to help keep your energy levels at a constant high, keeping you in a good mood and alert.

Power Snacking

Power snacking is something that really comes in handy for someone who works a job that requires them to use more muscle than brains. Depending on the type of job you hold, a mid-morning snack isn't always necessary, especially if you spend eight hours sitting behind a desk. Another reason why you may not need to power snack is, if you had a really good breakfast to fill you. If you were to eat a snack after a full breakfast, a couple hours later, all it would do to you is add extra calories to your daily diet. The only time a mid-morning snack really comes in handy is if you were either a person who never tends to have an appetite to eat in the mornings after waking up or if you are an early bird, who eats breakfast early in the morning.

Another way you could add a mid-morning snack to your meal plan is if you decide to have a really light lunch or dinner. Adding unnecessary calories to your diet is something that can really have a major effect on your alertness, the way your body functions, and also cause you to be lazy, tired, and sluggish.

Certain foods that contain too many unnecessary calories include sweets, such as danishes, cookies, glazed coffee rolls, etc. Consuming too many sugary pastries in the mornings can even cause terrible stomach aches, especially if that's the first thing that you want to put in your system early in the morning.

You see, what makes these foods bad for your health is the fact that they all consist of carbohydrates, high calories, and high fats, which is typical for most pastry treats. Even the so-called healthier varieties can contain hidden calories as well.

When it comes to being hungry, it seems almost as if you could just eat anything no matter what it is, even to the point that you may not care what it is as long as the stomach is fed. Right? Well, unfortunately this can sometimes lead to eating junk, and I mean lots of it.

One of the reasons for this may be because of the break time-limit that some of us have, and, yes, even I feel like I'm being challenged. What I do the night before is prepare my meals and healthy snacks that I could maybe snack on when I feel hungry. For example, I grab almonds by the bulk from any natural whole food store, because I know that they are not only delicious by themselves, but they can also be combined with dried fruits, seeds, or perhaps some chocolate chips. A little snack like this can also be hidden out of plain view for just in case you happen to be working a job that doesn't exactly allow you to eat while on the clock.

Almonds are considered to be a hard working snack, because they are packed with nutrients, such as fiber, Vitamin E, and even make a great source of protein, which can help you maintain a healthy cholesterol level too.

I have said this plenty of times, and I will say it again: if you want to enjoy your day with a good amount of energy, it is extremely important that you do so by starting off with a good breakfast. Another time that a power snack can really come in handy is if you happen to be one of those people who just simply cannot have an appetite to eat as soon as you wake up in the mornings. They, you can have a snack without feeling guilty at all. This is typical amongst many people, especially those who wake up super early in the morning.

The main part you would have to really be sure to do is that whatever type of breakfast you eat it is nourishing. Eating a well-nourishing, mid-morning snack can do the trick of holding a person over until they have lunch. If you decide to skip having a mid-morning snack, even though you have not had breakfast, and then wait until lunch time to eat, this can spell disaster. You may not care about what you eat at lunchtime and how much food you will consume in one sitting, which is another common mistake some super early morning people do, including those who don't have to wake up as early to go to work. Often times, these people who do this tend to find themselves so hungry by the time lunch comes around that they don't even realize that what they are doing is completely bad for their health. They are creating a habit of overeating and that will cause the experience of feeling sluggish and effecting their brain functioning.

To be on the safe side, it is always best to eat an adequate breakfast at the right time. That way, you do not really have to power snack in the mid-morning. If you feel the urge to eat, but also want to watch your physique as well, sip on liquids, such as tea, coffee, fruit juices, or, even better, water. If the urge to have a mid-morning snack is too strong to fight, then choose something that is low in fat. For example, if you had cereal, eggs, and orange juice for breakfast, when choosing your mid-morning snack, choose and some whole wheat peanut butter crackers., The best choice for a mid-morning snacks is vegetables, because they can be enjoyed with just about any food you want to eat. Try some sweet peppers and hummus or celery with peanut butter. Fruits and even yogurt are good choices as well.

THE POWER LUNCH

Lunch is an important meal that comes in handy, because it is eaten just at the right time that the energy levels that are obtained from eating breakfast in the morning begin to decrease. Once energy levels decrease, so does mental and physical energy.

A lunch that is rich in nutrients is what I consider to be known as a power lunch, because that is what it pretty much gives you: plenty of power to continue the day, especially brain power to help keep you focused. A well nutritious lunch also helps the body to produce chemical changes that can help you stay really alert and well responsive, feeling better than you might have felt before.

Below are some examples of some of the foods that can definitely give you the energy that you need. A fun way is to incorporate new ideas or tips to keep eating interesting for each day of the week.

MONDAY:

Cut boneless chicken thighs into1/2 inch chunks and add some salt and pepper. Make sure that you are originally cutting them from a five ounce piece of chicken. You can also do this with other types of meat, such as fish, because there are so many different varieties to choose from to make different tasty dishes. Beef is another type of meat you can be able to use, but keep it to minimum.

One thing you should avoid doing when cooking these meats is frying them. Instead, it is best to broil, bake, or grill it.

Once the meat is ready to be eaten, throw it on a wheat burger bun or regular wheat bread with lettuce, tomatoes, mustard, and take it easy on the mayonnaise. Or, better off, avoid it if you can.

Tuesday:

Try having a grilled shrimp salad. Start off with 1 cup of shrimp, four cups of green salad, ½ cup of white or red onions, one diced medium mixed vegetables to freshen up the smell and the taste of your lunch, and include three caps full of light Italian dressing to go with your grilled shrimp salad.

Wednesday:

Create a bowl of spicy chicken stir fry. Prepare it by adding 2 tsp of peanut oil, ½ medium cut onion, ½ cup of sliced carrots, 1/3 cup of black beans, 1/3 cup of asparagus tips, 1 boneless, skinless chicken breast cut into tiny pieces. Finish it off with 2 tsp of low sodium soy sauce, and voila!

Thursday:

Make yourself a pastrami sandwich by starting off with two whole wheat deli buns, 2 slices of beef pastrami, 2 slices of thin white onions, 2 pickles sliced to thin pieces, 2 slices of thin provolone cheese, 1 cup of green lettuce, 2 tsp of Dijon mustard, and 1 tsp of light mayonnaise. You now have yourself a really delicious pastrami sandwich, ready to be eaten.

Friday:

Have a vegetarian night! Stir fried bok choy with tofu. Start off with three large bok choy stalks, add 2 cups of firm tofu, 2 cups of corn starch, 1 shallot, 1 tsp of vegetable oil,1 tsp of oyster sauce,1/2 tbsp of salt. Cut the shallots into thin slices. Set the skillet on high heat. Add the 1 tsp of vegetable oil and the shallots and bok choy. Rotate the skillet to coast each side of leaves. Add 2 cups of tofu, and then cook it for one minute. Turn it only one time. Make sure that the tofu is really well coated. Add some oyster sauce to bring out the flavor.

Don't forget to continue stirring the tofu so that every bit of it remains coated. Then stir it for a minimum of 1 to 2 minutes, and cover it, letting it cook for 1 minute before removing it from the skillet. The stir fried bok choy and tofu is now ready to be served. It can be eaten over brown rice or quinoa.

The key to a productive day
is to eat a high energy, power
packed breakfast.

CHAPTER 8

BREAKING BAD EATING HABITS

Most of us just love to eat and only look at the urge to eat as being simple. Once we get hungry, we begin looking for food. As soon as we are full, the desire to eat stops. But this only satisfies for a short time and then it needs to be repeated a few hours later, especially in regards to junk food.

Researchers, from the burgeoning field food psychology, have found a complex web of cues in our environment that just overwhelm our systems. There include the distraction effects of watching television while eating, the bright colors that all food packages have, and big portion sizes.

Most of us don't notice, but we are often confronted with food decisions. It is said that the average American makes more than 200 hundred choices every day, mostly bad ones. However, there are some companies out there that want to lead us toward healthier diets, hoping to not only save lives, but to also avoid spending a lot of money in medical costs from today's obesity epidemic.

The goal is to rebuild the way you eat so that you can enjoy it without obsessing. Eating less junk food should be one of your goals as well. Try consuming five fruits and vegetables a day to increase your intake of fiber and Omega—3 fats.

In order to better understand how the psychology of food influences us, we must try to avoid being blinded by it and add more luster to foods that our bodies really need.

Breaking bad eating habits is possible. Learn to make good choices. Replace bad food choices with good ones. And, every once in a while, live a little.

What to Do About Sugar Cravings

Whenever you get a craving for dessert, remember two things: physique and health. This is something a lot of us don't think about, especially when the urge is so tempting. Sweets are a most common favorite, and not a lot of people can hold themselves back from ever enjoying such a thing.

I hate to admit it, but I'm definitely a sweets fan. I've found a new and better solution to enjoy a sweet snack any time I get a craving. When I need to go grocery shopping, I just take the time to sit down and write a list of all the natural, healthy, sweet things that I could possibly enjoy without having any regrets after eating it.

For example, "creamy vanilla ice cream" instead of buying the regular kind I'll buy myself the fat-free version. I usually have a bowl topped off with blueberries, natural unsalted almonds, and sundried raisins.

Now, keep in mind that ice cream isn't the only thing on my list. Veggies, chicken breast, brown rice, and any other healthy, natural food that I might need are on there too. You'll be surprised to find out that you can still enjoy the foods you like to eat, but with a substitution. There are plenty of healthy foods to choose from. However, you just have to make a commitment to change your eating behavior. Out with the old, in with the new.

All Natural Sugar: Fruit

Fruits are so much healthier for you than a regular sized bag of candy. Not only are fruits healthier, they are also delicious too. Fruits are naturally sweet, colorful, high in vitamins and fiber, and also low in calories and fat. If you eat 1 or 2 servings of fruit a day, it can reduce your susceptibility to many diseases.

Fruits are rich in antioxidants, Vitamin C, and phytochemicals, including antioxidants. Antioxidants also help destroy harmful substances in your body known as free radicals, which can build and lead to cancer. There are two types of phytochemicals—flavonoids and polyphenols, which together make up a very powerful antioxidant quality. Other phytochemicals in fruits have been found to be antiallergenic, anticarcinogenic, antiviral, and anti-inflammatory.

If 1 to 2 servings of fruit isn't enough, then try having a 2 to 4 servings daily. Fruits can also be enjoyed with a normal sized bowl of low-fat yogurt, mixed fruit salad, fruit smoothie, or low-fat cheese and fruit.

INCREASING YOUR INTAKE OF FRUIT

Fruits are a perfect alternative for candy and other artificial unnecessary sweets. They can come in many varieties and colors. Not only are they healthy and delicious, they also make great snacks. Because they don't need to be prepared, it makes them easier for taking to work or wherever it is that you are planning to be throughout the day. When taking in fruits, you should eat at least 3 to 4 servings a day. This is also good for promoting good health.

Some people are actually not very fond of fruit, just the way that there are non vegetable lovers. The best way to get into the habit of eating fruit is to start off by having one small piece of fruit, and then gradually add two more pieces. After a while, you will be so much into the groove of things that you might not even notice that you are doing it. Before then, you, too, will be meeting your daily requirement intake of fruit.

Fruits are very easy to add to meals and can be eaten any time of the day. Breakfast, lunch, dinner, and snacktime.

HERE ARE SOME EXAMPLES OF WAYS TO ADD FRUIT TO YOUR MEALS:

In the morning, you should have a bowl of cereal topped with some sliced fruit of your choice. I always prefer to eat my bowl of cereal with sliced banana and raisins.

For lunch, I have a regular bowl of brown rice and some mixed veggies. To keep myself from starving, I opt on snacking on two pieces of fruit instead of indulging on junk food. My, preferred choices are apples, peaches, strawberries, and oranges.

For snacks, as funny as this may sound, sometimes, when I am really hungry and cooking something healthy, depending on the cooking time of whatever I am preparing, I would always fix myself a banana sandwich made with wheat bread, and if I got hungry again, I would make another one until it was finally time to eat.

For some people, it might be too much. I choose to eat small snacks sometimes before a meal so that I do not starve and wander off into eating junk, which could really ruin your meal plan.

For dinner, I usually never get too fancy. I try to be as simple as possible, depending on how I feel. I might try something a little exotic, such as a grilled chicken caeser salad, mixed with a few slices of green apples or mango.

If that's still not enough, and my hunger continues, before I go to bed, I usually throw down a protein shake made of non-fat milk, banana, raisins, cantaloupe, and two scoops of peanut butter. Then I am off to bed.

Not Liking Vegetables

Part of breaking bad habits may even go back as far as habits formed in childhood. Maybe eating fruit hasn't been a problem for you. Perhaps it is vegetables that are your nemesis.

I am sure when you were little, you might have heard that carrots are good for you. Not only that, but also that they are good for your eye sight. I have heard this numerous of times, even mixed stories on how much of a lie it probably was, and that info was just given to kids so that they would eat their vegetables.

I am going to be honest with you. When I was a kid, I hated vegetables, especially carrots. I couldn't even stand the way they looked, smelled, or taste. I just figured that they were not for me, and maybe I could just live without them.

Of course, with my parents, primarily my father, I could never win. It was either I ate my vegetables like a good little boy so that one day I can grow up to be a strong young man or no dessert. Of course, being so little, I considered sweets as my best friend. Isn't that the way most kids look at it?

I saw two perfect opportunities. Eat my vegetables equaled grow muscles and enjoy my desert. But that still didn't take away my hatred for the way they tasted and smelled. So, from then on, I ate all vegetables by holding my nose.

Now, when I look back into the past, I laugh. Not all kids have a natural hatred for carrots, let alone vegetables. Well, not my daughter, for all I know. Around her, carrots or any vegetables don't stand a chance. She eats them with no questions asked. Now that's my little girl.

When Cravings Attack

There are many people who are interested in getting in shape, but many don't seem to realize this: it is said that our taste buds may be our worst enemy. Hunger has an ability to increase our taste sensitivity to sweet and salty substances, especially bad ones.

Take a vending machine for instance. Any snack that comes out of it can come in two flavors: sweet or salty. And, often, these are the types of snacks that end up being on the emergency menu when hungry, making a person that is extremely hungry believe that food is what tastes the best at the moment.

This is something that you want to try to avoid all together. Instead, try eating healthier foods regularly during the day to fight off these nasty cravings. When you crave sweets, eat a piece of fruit. When you crave salty, eat a vegetable snack.

Drink a glass of water, and wait 20 minutes. More than likely, those pesky cravings will subside, you'll feel revived, and you can continue your day full of energy and without any guilt.

Chapter 9

Eating Out Without Guilt

Some people may think just because their goal is to lose weight that they automatically have this conception that they have to stay away from eating out. That is not the case. Live a little! By choosing wisely that is.

Fast Food Ambiance and the Five Senses

Did you know that one of food's most seductive additives is the setting in which it's served? In addition to how the food tastes, what you see, smell, hear, and feel can affect the food choices that you make.

Fast food chains also understand how critical ambience is to make sales. Depending on how an establishment wants to make its sales, the choice of atmosphere differs. For example, at a fast food restaurant, profits depend on fast eating, while high-end restaurants tend to want you to stay longer so that they could bring up there sales by trying to sell you extra appetizers, desserts, and more drinks.

Color is another common technique that is used to achieve both goals. For example, the color red is known to stimulate a person's appetite. It also increases your adrenaline and blood pressure and makes you want to move. There are some restaurants that still uses the color red to stimulate appetites, but sometimes, they tone the color down to more like a wine or burgundy color. To top things off, they also use dim lights and relaxing music just to get you feeling as comfortable as possible.

People are particularly vulnerable to manipulations, such as bright lights, loud noises, and reflective surfaces. This can sometimes cause most of us to eat faster.

Environmental stimulation can cause men to speed up their eating, because it has an exaggerated influence.

Smell is another highly provocative sense. Just a quick whiff of something that smells really delicious will increase salivation and the release of pancreatic enzymes, getting our bodies ready to be fed.

The textures of certain foods, chairs you sit in, and even the feel of the napkin in your hand or lap—all these things can affect the way you choose to eat.

Dining Out Tips and Tricks

With so many choices to make being constantly aware of good choices vs. bad is essential. Follow the below tips and drinks to increase your chances for healthy dining out success.

Tip #1: Eat a snack ahead of time.

The best way to ensure that everything works out is to snack on something, such as an apple or two before going out to the restaurant that you plan to go to. This prevents you from being really hungry and overeating or ordering unnecessary appetizers, including bread.

Tip #2: Stop eating as soon as you are full.

Once you get full, stop eating. Just in case there is more food remaining on the plate, have it removed by the waitress that happens to be bussing your table.

Tip #3: Stick to the one glass rule.

With any alcoholic beverage that you order, stick just to that one glass. Sip on it rather than gulping it down. Make it last as long as possible. Even certain alcoholic beverages can be high in sugars and other unhealthy, added preservatives. Sometimes, drinking a lot of alcohol will lead you to being thirsty. Do not drink any more. Drink water to better quench your thirst.

Tip #4: Banish the bread basket.

Avoid eating whatever leftover bread is in the basket that happens to be on the table. Another way to make sure that you do not eat any of it, just tell the waiter or waitress that you do not want any.

Tip #5: Say no to sauces.

The less oil, butter, or sauce that comes with the meal, the better. Or, better yet, ask for your meal to be served to you without it to be on the safe side.

Some may get frustrated with all the choices to make. But, stay vigilant. Don't just shrug and order a salad. Be aware of what you're eating at all times. Sometimes, a salad isn't just a salad.

Salad Dos and Don'ts

Although you have already heard me say this plenty of times throughout the book, I will continue to do so until I get the point across: Foods that are high in both fat and calories are bad for your health. They will get in the way of your mental performance, physical activity, and your mental strength. You may be surprised to find out that despite how careful you are about how much fat you consumed, mainly because most of the hidden in certain ingredients that are in so-called low calorie meals, you're still consuming more fat than you should be.

Let me use one of my friends as an example. He likes to go out to a health food restaurant located in downtown Boston. I remember having a conversation with him regarding what type of foods he should consider adding to his diet for obtaining energy throughout the day and which ones not to eat. When I asked him about what he had for lunch, his response was a salad—not bad for a start. Now, I expected there to be more to the salad that he had for lunch, which there was. Unfortunately, I was not prepared to hear what he had with that salad. His response was he usually adds many things, such as creamy ranch dressing, 4 sliced boiled eggs, yolk and all, a fried chicken breast, sliced to strips, a hand full of cubed, bite-sized, American cheese, a slice of buttered bread on the side, and a large side Coke. To top things off, he also finishes his meal with a piece of cake on his way back to work. Not surprisingly, he mentioned that he always felt extremely tired and sluggish. Talk about fattening, huh?

So, finally, I had enough. And decided to step in and make a few corrections. I made it clear to him that if he was going to continue working as a personal trainer, he could not go on eating the way he does. Although he had the right foundation for eating healthy by having a salad for lunch, it is what he put on it that killed the word healthy. Something just had to be done. If he wanted his clients to look up to him, it was going to start that day.

What I told him was to keep the salad and add mixed raw vegetables to it. Keep the chicken, but make it grilled instead of fried. Add 2 tablespoons of fat-free salad dressing. Get rid of the slice of buttered bread, and switch the coke for fruit juice or water. Forget about the piece of cake, and if necessary, choose a piece of fruit instead.

Once he took my advice, there were no more feelings of tiredness. Instead, his energy levels were a lot higher than it was the day before, which made him feel like a newer person and enabled him to concentrate on his clients at peak performance. Because of my advice, he now eats in the manner that a personal trainer should eat and occasionally, he comes to me for help whenever he needs it.

You know what cracks me up? When a person aims to eat healthy, knows exactly what foods to eat, but for some reason they always forget that just because you are eating healthy foods, once you begin to add way too many extras, it can also become a fattening meal. This too can become a trap. So even when you may think that you are doing your body good, you may end up doing the total opposite.

I always find myself correcting those people on their food flaws, especially when it comes to eating salads. I don't mind giving other people the right advice on what type of foods that may benefit their health. Usually I may warn them about how much salad dressing or any added extras they should be using and guide them to eating more vegetables and add more protein instead. This catches them by surprise whenever I tell them that what they are consuming isn't always going to be good for them.

Just because it's a salad, many people can get confused. A salad is only healthy and good for you when you add the right things to it. Don't drench your lettuce in half a bottle of dressing or any of the other additives that are usually added to trick people into thinking that they are doing the right thing. Instead, add just three cap full's of dressing of the non-fat variety of what you would normally use on a salad.

What makes a salad also nutritious is when it is prepared with grilled chicken or any kind of other source of protein foods available, including raw vegetables. If the vegetables are cooked, the chances of vitamins and nutrients that you should be obtaining could be drained out of them. If that's the case, you might as well drink the water they were cooked in.

Whatever you do, don't fall into the thinking that just because you are eating a salad for lunch, but decide to add all types of extras to it, that it's still going to remain a healthy meal. It isn't. A truly nutritious salad is supposed to be low in fat and light, even on the dressing, get it?

A salad doesn't always have to be made up of lettuce. There are other varieties out there that are ready for you to enjoy as well. The only two that I know of which you should stay away from are both potato salad and macaroni salad, due to the high content of mayonnaise, which, in turn, is very high in fat.

HEALTHY EATING AND ETHNIC FOODS

Many people have a taste for foods from different ethnic backgrounds. I am one of them. What make these foods so special is the types of spices and herbs that are used to cook them with, how good they smell, and how delicious they taste when ready to be served.

Look, let's face it. Both you and I know how hard it is to stay focused on what right foods we should really be consuming. Just about wherever you go there are always going to be different restaurants that represent food from all over the world with their own unique taste fit for every individual's taste.

Sometimes, you may stumble upon these places while traveling, whether it's for work-related purposes or simply for pleasure. What makes things difficult is when restaurants that serve healthy foods are either hard to come by or, worse, non-existent, and they, oftentimes, can leave you with no choice but to answer to hunger's call with whatever you find handy. You know, when that happens, the power of hunger can make you forget the foods you should really be eating. Does this sound familiar to you?

It happened to me when I used to compete. I used to also travel a lot because most of the shows that I attended were never local. Although I would always pack my lunch with extra food, for some reason, it was never enough. You see, these body building shows consist of two events: the prejudging show and the night show. These are for the top five people who qualified to compete that night. Luckily for me, when my food ran out, it always happened after I have competed in the morning show.

Not to sound like I am bragging or anything, but I was usually lucky to make it in the top five, and when I did, I still tried to keep myself in the condition I was in when I came in that morning, which meant that I couldn't celebrate just yet. I knew sooner or later I was going to get hungry, and I did.

The place where I was staying had a restaurant and served the type of foods that I used to prepare my meals, but it was the way those foods were cooked that had me worried. I didn't want to eat the wrong foods. If I did, I would look horrible on stage, which could cost me a placing. However, I still had to eat, or else I would have gone flat, which would still make me look bad.

Then, it finally dawned on me: "Chinese food". What if I went to a local Chinese food restaurant, and I ordered just a small side of steamed vegetables and plain shrimp? To me, these were the best choices out of what these places would usually serve. When I went with my inner gut feeling, I didn't feel bad at all.

To make a long story short, I did go on to win in my weight class, the overall class, and then overall.

Although everyone can't relate to being a bodybuilder, we all do have something in common when it comes to watching what you eat at ethnic restaurants and while traveling. Even when you feel trapped with a situation of really great foods that are just out of the healthy eating league, just go for the best foods out of the worst, with less fat and calories, so that you do not leave with a guilty feeling of messing up your diet.

FAST FOOD TRAPS

Other so called healthy meals, such as chicken sandwiches from fast food restaurants can also put you into a food trap because of the white bread, cheese, and ketchup, which also has a pretty high content of sodium when you add more than one package.

When I want to have fast food I plan it for every other weekend and bring my own whole wheat burger buns. Even when I order a burger, I always request that they not add mayonnaise, cheese, or ketchup. I never ask for fries because of the amount of oil the contained, but I do ask for a medium cup to fill with sugar-free iced tea. That's pretty much it.

When some of my friends saw me at any fast food joint, it caught them by surprise. They immediately thought they had me cornered, until I showed them what I was doing and how I did it. I told them that you can always eat what you want, but the most important thing is that you have to know how to do it.

CHOOSING THE BEST OF THE WORST

When going out to a restaurant for food, you also have to be ready to know when to make the choice of sacrifice. Let's say that you went to a restaurant early in the morning to have breakfast, and the choices of breakfast foods that they had available were not what you would call healthy.

Depending on how much time you have on your hands, the best solution for dealing with this situation is knowing how to choose the best foods from the worst. What that means is, knowing which breakfast foods have the least amount of fat, calories, grease, sugar, and sodium.

One thing that I strongly urge you to do is a bit of homework on the kind of foods that they serve by asking for a take home menu if they have any readily available.

If you are able to ahead of time, many restaurants have website or nutritional value charts online that you can research. If not, know your foods. Obviously, fruit will be a better choice than hash browns; egg whites will be a better choice that pancakes; orange juice will be a better choice than a hot chocolate; and so on.

Other great choices also include plain wheat bread toast without any butter on it, and/or a cinnamon Danish or a bran muffin on the side, instead of any other kind of greasy bacon or home fries.

If you feel like having eggs that morning, ask for 5 egg whites and one whole egg either scrambled or boiled, but never fried. If you cannot do without the butter, try to limit the use of it to just a little bit and easy on the salt. If you want to have those eggs with a side of bacon or sausage, don't do it. Go for a slice of lean ham or turkey bacon.

THE ALLURE OF FAST FOOD & ALL-YOU-CAN-EAT BUFFETS

If you are among those trying to lose weight and also want to achieve the fit muscular look and maintain it, then limiting frequent visits to fast food restaurants, all-you-can-eat buffets, Chinese food takeouts, and any other fast food spots should be one of the major things that you should work on first.

Very few people will order more than they can actually eat, especially at all-you-can-eat buffets. Who in the world can resist grabbing a piece of their favorite dessert? Creamy vanilla ice cream, coconut cream pie, and all the other sweet stuff that isn't on the healthy list laid out directly in front of you, can be difficult to pass by, even for the strongest of dieters. Plus, many people want to make sure that they "get their money's worth", which cause them to overeat.

If you're already managing to keep bad foods out of your diet, then more power to you. Keep up the good work. The next time you happen to be at a buffet, try to limit yourself to at least two items on the plate. You can always go back for seconds. But, establishing a buffet zone between all the food choices will calm the allure, making it much easier to control yourself.

Have ever picked up a menu at a restaurant and noticed the name of a certain appetizer or dish, but you couldn't pronounce it correctly? When we read these names, we expect something special, and we even end up thinking they taste better. For some reason, they have an ability to evoke our emotions, giving us the desire to want.

A description of great taste is a common tactic, and it can make our mouths water and stomachs growl as effectively as actual food. From pizza, garlic bread, and cheese or perhaps just a plain fat juicy steak, just thinking about food is enough for our imaginations to make it actually happen.

Companies also use are brand names. You can actually fight the urge by simply being more conscious of certain foods that you are surrounded by. Here is a sample products that can be bad for you: salt, corn syrup, artificial flavors, lactose, milk fat, partially hydrogenated soybean oil, peanuts, milk chocolate, chocolate, milk-fat, egg whites, sugar, soy lecithin. All of these foods when looked at by themselves aren't that appealing. But, when you realize that they are the ingredients in a delicious Snickers bar, you may be more inclined to want to eat one.

Being aware and staying alert to these types of tricks and methods that food companies use, can help you to make better decisions when going out . . . or, better yet, choose to make a delicious and healthy meal at home with your favorite healthy foods. You can't go wrong there!

Easy Recipes for Your Own Week's Lunch Menu

Compared to restaurant menus that you are accustomed to seeing, I have come up with my version of the food menu. The obvious difference is unlike the traditional food menu that you would normally see at an everyday restaurant, my version will not list foods that are high in fat or calories. Instead, it represents a whole week's worth of foods that can make perfect lunches that are also low in fat, high in protein, and even low in calories. These foods that I have included are in fact much healthier for you not only for the time being, but for the long run as well.

#1) Cottage Cheese and Cornbread Muffin

1 cup of low low-fat cottage cheese, mixed with 1 cup of sliced peaches or any fruit of your choice.1 whole grain cornbread muffin, and 8 ounces of low-fat or fat-free milk.

#2) Chili

1/12 cup of chili, 1 package of saltine crackers, 1 cup of raw broccoli or any vegetable of your choice, and 8 ounces of low-fat or fat-free milk.

#3) Tuna Salad Sandwich

3 ounces of mixed tuna with chopped chives, scallions, celery, and sprinkle of lemon juice on top. Add 1 tablespoon of fat-free mayonnaise.Place the tuna mixture on two slices of whole grain bread with 1 tablespoon of olive oil, 2 cups of green lettuce, and 1 cup of medium sliced of cucumber and carrots. Finish with 1/12 teaspoon of light vinegar oil or Italian low-fat dressing. Enjoy with a side cup of 8 ounces of low-fat or fat-free milk.

#4) Chicken Pita Sandwich

4 ounces of sliced, skinless chicken breast, 2 slices of whole grain pita bread, 2 tablespoons of mustard or mayonnaise. Pair with 1 piece of fruit and 8 ounces of low-fat or fat-free milk.

#5) Egg Salad Sandwich

2 hard boiled eggs with 2 slices of whole grain wheat bread, and 2 teaspoons of mayonnaise, a medium bowl of mixed fruit, and 8 ounces of low-fat or fat-free milk.

#6) Roast Beef Roll

3 ounces of lean roast beef, 2 slices of whole grain bread roll, 1 medium sliced tomato, ¾ cup of sherbet, and 8 ounces of low-fat or fat-free milk.

#7) Greek Salad

2 cups of lettuce, 3 ounces of feta cheese, ½ cup of beets, 1 or 2 teaspoon of fat-free dressing, a small piece of pita bread, 1 cup of mixed fresh fruit, and 8 ounces of low-fat or fat-free milk.

Don't those recipes sound better than fast food anyways? Keeping your menu fun and creative throughout the week can make all the difference in staying committed and on track with your eating for energy goals.

Chapter 10

Protein for Power

How Protein Works

Protein is an essential component of successful muscle building diet. It drives the muscle to grow, especially amino acids. The building blocks or subunits of protein increase the production of hormones in the body that affect muscle repair. Eating a good amount of protein leads to elevated levels of amino acids in the blood stream. That is correlated with higher growth hormone and insulin-like growth factors I levels.

Growth hormone supports size expansion by pushing amino acids into muscles and sparing the breakdown of muscle tissue, while IGFI is more like HGH, it signals the muscle cells to grow while raising hormone levels, the amino acids trigger the muscle size increases by signaling muscle cells to turn on the muscle building process, known as protein synthesis.

Protein contains 22 amino acids that are necessary for building and repairing healthy tissue as well as minerals, vitamins, fatty acids, and natural detoxifying agents. Protein also decreases hunger when you eat a meal high in protein. It's also best to consume a good amount of protein at every meal to keep your muscles nourished, especially if you are weight training or doing any other kind of active sport. Otherwise, your muscles will turn and cannibalize themselves. Protein is an essential nutrient, because it keeps your body strong. Like fiber and fat, it also stops the production of insulin by slowing the digestion of food. The slower the food is digested, the more our blood sugar levels rise and the slower the production of insulin. This is one major reason why a high protein diet is so important and effective at dropping body fat.

It also raises hormone levels, blunting hormones that are released by the digestive tract and tells the brain that you are full. This can also help to decrease your cravings and keep you on track while you are dieting to get lean. Protein also works with carbohydrates. Although carbohydrates can cause the levels of insulin to increase, combining fast digestive protein, such as whey protein powder with carbohydrates can really exert a strong up tick on insulin production. The combination also turns on mechanisms that drive creatine into the muscles. The best form of protein to buy should be a type of whey that is low in fats and carbohydrates.

The Importance of Metabolic Pathways

Metabolic pathways are what help the body while it is using the amino acids, vitamins, and minerals by transforming the proteins and using them in many ways. A certain type of amino acid is used by the body to put together an RNA pattern for it to become part of a type of molecule called a fibrous protein molecule.

It can also go through various changing stages while interacting with many different enzymes, vitamins, and minerals so that it changes to another amino acid.

Amino acids are used depending on how your body needs it. For example, if your body wants to make some digestive enzymes, it will connect or maybe transform the right amount of amino acids it needs. This also goes for hormones, skeletal muscles, antibodies, connective tissues, blood vessels, and other structures that make up the interior of the body.

THE ROLES PROTEIN PLAYS

Proteins are part of the enzymes and hormonal systems. They also make up antibodies. Not only do they build and repair muscles, they also build NLEO proteins known as DNA and RNA, which also transport oxygen while building muscle tissue.

Both DNA and RNA are what make up the structure of all living organisms, and they are the main materials that the body uses to continue living.

Amino acids are also important because they help vitamins and minerals do what they have to do for the body. Although vitamins and minerals are absorbed and assimilated properly, their potency would depend on the amino acids presence.

There are 22 amino acids that the body depends on for making protein. They are known as non-essential amino acids, which makes up of 14. These non-essential amino are the following: alagine, aspotic acid, carnitine, cysteine, glutamic acid, glutamine, glycine, histidine, proline, serine, taurine, and tyrosine.

The essential aminos are the following: lysine, leucine, isoleucine, methionine, phenylalanine, threonine. Tryptophon and valine.

Although there has been 100 amino acids that were identified, since amino acids are divided into two categories, they are misleading.

Amino acids have a very powerful influence on the physiological system, which also means it is important to have all 22. They are crucial for the body to have for constructing the molecules that compose it. Without these amino acids the body can't be able to repair or rebuild itself the way it needs to.

Also, without the presence of amino acids, the body won't be able to manufacture more of it to meet the demands, especially when the amino acids are needed. The body will also break down the muscle tissue that already exists, especially if one of the amino acids is in short supply.

MUSCLE-BUILDING PROTEINS

There are people who are highly against putting supplements in their body, especially when trying to build muscle or simply just to stay healthy but prefer to get their daily nutrients from natural foods. Part of this is probably because of a fear of dependency and the extra additives that some supplements could contain. I don't blame you. After all, the natural way is healthier and a lot safer.

If you are among those people who much rather not use supplements for any of those reasons, but would prefer to get your nutrients from natural foods, then here are 8 muscle building foods to help you put on muscle: Eggs, almonds, olive oil, salmon, steak, yogurt, chicken, and turkey.

By adding these ingredients to your diet and training faithfully and heavily, you should have no problem with growing a pair of super biceps.

EGGS

Eggs contain the highest biological value of protein, compared to beef. You would need less protein from eggs then you do from other sources in order to achieve the same muscle building benefits. You would also have to eat the yolk.

Eggs also contain Vitamin B12, which is also important for the breaking down of fat and muscle contraction. They also keep you healthy, because they are packed with iron, phosphorus, zinc, riboflavin, folate, and Vitamins B6, B12, D, and E.

ALMONDS

Almonds are considered to be one of the best sources of alphatocopherol Vitamin E. This form is best absorbed by your body. Vitamin E is important to your muscles, because it is a potent antioxidant that can help prevent free radical damage after each heavy workout.

In order for the use of almonds to be really potent, it is best to consume two big handfuls a day. Almonds are also good for you because they do not cause weight gain and can also help you be at a lower risk for Alzheimer's disease than those who consume a lesser amount of Vitamin E.

Olive Oil Olive oil is high in monosaturated fat, and it is also good for the prevention of muscle breakdown by lowering levels of a sinister cellular protein, known as tumor necrosis factor-a. This is also linked with the wasting of muscle and muscle weakening. Olive oil and monounsaturated fats are also associated with lowering the risk of heart disease, colon cancer, osteoporosis, and diabetes.

SALMON

Salmon is packed with high quality protein and Omega-3 fatty acids. Omega-3's also help to decrease the breaking down of muscle protein after your workout and improving recovery.

In order to build muscle, you would need to store new protein even faster than your body could break down the protein that's already there. If you add 1.8g of Omega-3 fatty acid to your daily diet, it can help you reduce the risk of diabetes and heart disease, and if someone with diabetes were to also consume the same amount of Omega-3 as another person without diabetes, then their insulin resistance would decrease by 70 percent in 12 weeks.

STEAK

Although there are some of us see steak as just a piece of steak for barbecuing, it also provides two types of muscle building nutrients: iron and zinc. It's also a number one food source for getting the creatine that your body needs for weightlifting.

That means you would at least be getting 2g for every 16 ounces. It's said that for a maximum amount of muscle gain with minimum calories, it's best to buy the rounds or the loin parts of the steak. You also could just buy the flat iron cut, because it's very lean and also supposed to be the second tenderest cut of beef overall.

YOGURT

Believe it or not yogurt is another good type of muscle builder because it has a combination of protein and carbohydrates. This is helps your muscles recover and grow after exercise. It's best to buy regular yogurt with fruit and not the sugar free kind.

Yogurt with fruit contains extra carbohydrates that boost your blood levels of insulin. This is also one of the main keys for reducing post exercise protein breakdown. Yogurt also contains conjugated linoleic acid, also known as CLA. This is a special type of fat that's also known to help reduce body fat.

CHICKEN

It's best to consume 8—12 ounces, 2 to 3 servings of chicken daily. Chicken is also better for you when consumed baked or grilled, and not fried. You can also add it to a nice crisp bowl of lettuce and veggies, and then top it off with any low-fat dressing of your choice. Quickly and easily, you'll be enjoying a healthy and delicious chicken salad.

Chicken is a form of white meat that is good for putting on muscle and a good source of low-fat protein. It's also low in saturated fat. To minimize the saturated fat content of chicken, or any other type of poultry, like turkey, you can either grill, bake, or broil the meat and remove the skin before consuming.

DIFFERENT SOURCES OF PROTEIN

Protein is a very important nutrient that the body needs. It can be obtainable from many sources of food. However, the body does not store it, so, therefore, we must take in this nutrient every day. Some people look at this as something that should be consumed once a day, depending on what their needs are, which is usually ok. However, not everybody takes in the same source of protein. Some are vegetarians, where they only get their sources from plants for a daily intake of protein. Proteins come in different varieties, such as bens, lentils, nuts, seeds, peas, poultry, beef and fish.

Unlike the protein sources that come from animals, protein from plants do not contain the type of amino acids that make up protein and would have to be put together in a form in order to be completed as a source of protein, except for soy. It contains more protein than legumes, and it has almost as much amino acids as proteins that come from animals.

Protein also can be obtained from milk, cheese, bread, eggs, and shellfish. However, not all protein has the same fat content. The purpose of protein is for help to make your muscles grow, regulate the metabolism, and repair tissue from damage after exercising.

Dietary Requirements of Protein

Everybody has their own dietary requirements on how much protein they need to take in daily, which goes by how much a person weighs, what the condition of their health is, and how much they need to eat. A person's body needs more protein to fight off sickness and when the body is in a lot of stress, which is also because the body uses up a lot of energy and makes protein important to have. The building blocks of protein are considered to be a type of amino acid that the immune system depends on. It is important that a person takes in a good amount of protein. Without the body receiving a good supply of this nutrient, the muscles could go into waste, and you could suffer from malnutrition.

Women need it the most when they are pregnant, which means their intake goes up by 30g per day, and when breast feeding, they should take 20g of protein per day. However, it is even more important for children to consume plenty of protein, because they need it more than adults to keep them growing. They should be taking in 2.2g of protein per 2.2lb (1kg) for the other half of the six months. After a child begins to grow, their daily requirements begin to decrease to 8g per 22lb (1hg) per day, until they are 18 years of age. Athletes, in general, have different requirements of protein that they need. Some may go as far as thinking the more protein they consume, the more muscle mass they will put on.

The protein you use will either be used as energy, if the intake of calories or carbohydrates is low, or waste turned into fat. Just like carbohydrates, protein is a nutrient that should be carefully balanced. You can't eat too little or too much. Extra protein is only used when trying to lose unwanted weight. This should only be done if necessary and advised by a doctor a dietitian. Sometimes, extra consumption of protein over a long period of time can cause disease, kidney stones, or osteoporosis.

A person's recommended daily intake of protein is often calculated by what their body weight, gender, or height is. An adult should be taking in roughly around 0.8g of protein per 2.2lb (1kg) of body weight every day. For example, a man weighing in at 180 lbs should be consuming about 65g of protein a day, and a woman weighing in at 150 lbs should be consuming 55g of protein a day.

Power Protein: Lean Meats and Low-Fat Dairy

It is good to know that there are other varieties of meat to choose from, rather than just sticking to plain chicken or beef, which isn't always a favorite of every meat lover or vegetarian. These other varieties include boar, buffalo, elk, and venison, which all contain about the same amount of cholesterol as other red meat. Due to the extra amounts of exercise animals get, their meat is much lower in calories and fats.

These types of meats should be eaten in small moderations. There are also people who are big fans of eating other sections of animals, which can sometimes be high in cholesterol, such as tongue, tripe, kidney, and liver. Keep in mind that although these parts of the animal are high in cholesterol, they make good sources of Vitamins A, B, D, and E. Additionally, they also contain minerals, such as copper, iron, and zinc.

However, there is a big difference in what type of animal liver you choose to consume. For example, adult animal liver accumulates the residues, which make it much better to eat young animal liver instead. Even if you choose to eat young animal liver, it is still better to eat it once a week. It is also important that you avoid eating processed meat, such as beef sausage, deli meat, bacon, and pork, which are known to be the cause of cancer.

Better alternatives are soy or different variety meats that are low in fat and have no preservatives. The requiring serving of these types of meats are two or three a day, remember that red meat should be consumed only once a week, preferably lean cut meat. Example servings are, 3 ½ oz (100g) pork loin, 3 ½ oz (100-mg) sirloin steak, 3 ½ oz (100-mg) venison, 3 ½ oz (100-mg) ground beef, 3 ½ oz (100-mg) flank steak, 3 ½ oz(100-mg) round steak and 3 ½ oz(100-mg) filet mignon.

READY FOR RED MEAT?

Although there have been reports on how red meat and eating too much of it can cause cancer, some people still choose to eat the same excessive amounts that they were eating before. It is ok to eat red meat, but at a certain amount. Again, it is best to eat meats that are of lean cut variety, preferably pork loin and filet mignon. It is also best to cook these meats in healthier ways by trimming off all the excess fat, and then placing the piece of meat on a rack, preferably grilling, broiling, or baking it, not frying. As you do this, whatever amount of excess fat that remains will drip down into the pan, which is the part you throw away. Try not to use so much oil, you can also use nonfat cooking spray. Another good way to prepare these meats are with vegetables or salads.

When you to choose to eat out and have steak, try to limit how much of it you eat. Sometimes, if you order a big plate of steak and a side order, it might be best to share it with your girlfriend or whoever you happen to be out with.

Lean Meat Dinner for Two Recipe
12 oz (340g) beef
4 cups of brown rice
1 green pepper
1 tablespoon olive oil
1 small onion

Each serving contains 434 total fat, 8.8g saturated, 2.4g, poly 2.0g, momo 4.3g, 82-mg cholesterol, 42g protein, 80g carbohydrates, 17g fiber, 76-mg sodium, also contains, Vitamins A and C, and minerals calcium, magnesium, potassium, and selenium.

Although red meat is rich in protein, it is also extremely high in saturated fat. These meats include veal, beef, lamb, and pork. It is best to eat at least two servings of these sources of protein sparingly, preferably 2 to 3oz, which contain about 55 to 85g. However, many of us that are non-vegetarians tend to eat more than the proper required serving. People who eat more red meat all the time are more likely to be at risk of developing cardiovascular disease than those who eat the proper serving at the right time. The reason behind red meat causing cardiovascular disease is because of the high cholesterol and saturated fat it contains. Too much red meat also leads to development of colon cancer.

You have to keep in mind that there are other great sources of protein out there, you do not have to necessarily rely on just an intake of red meat all the time as your only source.

Other meats that are available are fish, such as tuna, salmon, and trout. Other sources include chicken. If you are not a fan of chicken, other choices of poultry are also available. Choosing fish, chicken, or other poultry sources can help lower the risk of developing cardiovascular disease and other health related disease, such as colon cancer. Honestly, the best thing to do for avoiding a brush with one of these illnesses is to rightfully choose one of the healthier protein sources mentioned above.

Low-fat vs. High-fat Proteins

Did you know that you can also benefit your health by choosing low-fat proteins besides the other high-fat varieties? Yes, this is true, just by choosing proteins that are low in fat, preferably lean protein, you will get greater amounts of it, weight for weight, especially animal protein that is rich in this stuff. Compare low-fat proteins to those of higher fat contents. For example, steak, is a low-fat protein that is a much better and healthier choice for ensuring that your heart stays healthy throughout life, which is the total opposite of what animal proteins of high fat would do. Protein with a higher fat percentage is also known to cause high blood cholesterol levels and lead to cardiovascular disease, Higher fat content protein is best to eat once or twice a month.

Don't forget low-fat or fat-free dairy products are also considered to be good sources of low-fat proteins too. Other good sources include egg whites, fish or shellfish, any type of poultry without the skin, and soy protein foods.

GETTING YOUR PROTEIN FROM DAIRY

If you eat a daily amount of 1,200 mg of calcium from dairy, you would lose about 24 pounds or maybe 12 percent of your body weight. When there isn't enough calcium in your diet, it causes you to be more efficient at making fat and less efficient at breaking it down, causing bigger fatter cells.

Milk is an important substance that is highly needed for the body. Dairy products are a very nutritional food. However, it would be best to avoid dairy that is of the full fat variety. Any low-fat or non-fat milk and the products that are made from it are good sources of protein and also contain calcium, vitamins, and minerals, which is also important for promoting healthy teeth and bones.

Milk, and the other products that derive from it, can have many options to choose from. Cow's milk is often the most common type of milk that is chosen in the United States. However, goat's milk as well as sheep's milk can be available.

Even milk that comes from certain plants, such as oat milk and soy milk are sometimes consumed.

When cow's milk is processed, it is done in many ways so that it creates different products that can vary in their own nutritional content and also in the different ways of storage life. There is a big difference between whole milk and low-fat and fat-free milk. For example, the fat content in the varieties of milk is one of the important differences, which can vary from whole milk that contains about 3.25% milk fat versus what the containing amount of milk fat is for low-fat and fat-free milk.

Products that are made from whole milk are usually high in saturated fats and cholesterol, which means that you should avoid that kind of stuff. But, wait. If you happen to love dairy products a lot because of how delicious and nutritional they are, then there is no need to worry. There are other healthier versions of whatever type of dairy product you might be interested in. However, sometimes, whatever you could be looking for may not be carried by your local supermarket. There is always a possibility of finding what you need, just as long as you look hard enough.

When choosing fat-free or low-fat dairy products, you are actually gaining more than you would be from consuming dairy with more saturated fats and cholesterol. The healthier varieties contain all the nutrients the body needs without you having to worry about the harmful ingredients added. Milk or any other form of dairy is a food that shouldn't be counted out of the healthy diet, especially yours. After all, "it does the body good".

When you are not getting enough, you should always bring the intake up. You should be choosing products that are low-fat or fat-free. By doing this, it ensures that you are not taking in unhealthy, saturated, bad fats.

The best thing about this food is that it can be enjoyed any time of the day; breakfast, lunch, dinner, and/or snack. For example, for breakfast, try having a Grape Nut type of cereal with a little bit of dried fruit and some low-fat milk. Or try some fat-free yogurt with a little bit of dried fruit. You can even try oatmeal with low-fat milk. But that's if you would rather do that without the water.

For lunch, add a glass of milk to a whole grain wheat Italian sub, minus the fattening fancy stuff. Instead, add some low-fat mayonnaise, lettuce, tomatoes, low-fat American cheese, sliced turkey, ham, and a little bit of fat-free Italian dressing.

For dinner, it might be best to have a baked sweet potato, mixed with vegetables sprinkled on top, with a little bit of fat-free cottage cheese.

For just in case you get hungry before bedtime, try fresh dried fruits with low-fat frozen yogurt.

I know that for some people, making a change in consuming regular dairy to fat-free dairy can be a bit of a challenge, especially if that's all you really grew up on. Believe me, this was the same problem I've once encountered. However, some of us learn to adapt better than others when it comes to making changes.

What you should do is gradually start bringing in one or two dairy products that are fat-free or low-fat while cutting back on regular full-fat dairy. Gradually, wean yourself from full-fat dairy products a little bit at a time. Try this process over and over again until you get used to it, then completely ditch the regular dairy products all together.

Choosing to go fat-free can also go good with certain Italian dishes, such as lasagna. Yummy! Delicious.

Milk for the Lactose Intolerant

Although it is highly important that many of us take in a certain daily intake of dairy products as part of our dietary needs, it is still important that everyone consumes what is right for them. For example, certain people may require taking in a special type of dairy product that is made specifically for them, especially when it comes to milk—due to their intolerance of lactose.

Milk can also come in dried powdered forms, condensed forms, and evaporated forms. These can also be used to cook up some very tasty dishes that may require the use of dairy.

VARIETIES OF HEALTHY DAIRY FOODS

There are many types of dairy products that are made from milk. These include yogurt, cream, butter, cream cheese, even variations of other cheeses and dairy products.

Cheese can contain the good source of the crucial nutrients found in milk, which is why it is so high in saturated fat. Cheeses can also come in reduced fat varieties so, so the ongoing enjoyment of cheese can continue without worries of consuming products that are high in saturated fat and cholesterol

RECOMMENDED DAIRY SERVINGS

It is probably obvious that, by now, you need to be paying attention to what you are eating and drinking as well as the daily recommended dosage, if you are still unsure it is ok.

To take in an adequate amount of dairy products, the recommended dosage should at least be between one to three servings daily. For example; 8 fl oz (240-ml) of lactose reduced low-fat milk, 8 fl oz (240 ml) enriched soy milk, 1 cup of low-fat frozen yogurt, 1 of cup vanilla ice cream, 8 fl oz (240 ml) of low-fat fruit yogurt, 1 cup of low-fat pudding, 8 fl oz (240 ml) of reduced fat 2%, low—fat 1%, or fat—free milk.

1 oz (28g) of part-skim mozzarella, 4 fl oz (120-ml) of low-fat cottage cheese, or 8 fl oz (240-ml) of fruit smoothie.

THE BENEFITS OF YOGURT

Yogurt has got to be one of the best consumable products out there. It comes from milk, which has been treated with a bacterial culture. This type of food can be enjoyed any time of the day, and it can be available in many different flavors and forms. Remember, reduced fat is the best way to go. Yogurt also contains active cultures that are very important for helping to keep the intestines healthy. Yogurt also contains riboflavin (B2), and it is also high in protein.

In addition to yogurt being so healthy, it is also very delicious. It also taste good when you throw a little bit of oat meal flakes on top. It also goes very well with dried fruit, dried nuts, or enjoyed by itself.

CHOOSE CHEESE

If you think yogurt is fun, try cheese!

Cheese is a food that is made from cow's milk, sheep's milk, or goat's milk. Cheese is made when the milk is heated with the enzyme called rennin. Rennin helps to separate the curds that are collected and then processed. The mix is then either curded or salted. The flavor and the texture of the cheese come from the curing. However, when the cheese is cured for a long time, its texture gets harder, while the flavor gets stronger.

Cheese and milk both share the same equivalence of nutritional value. Regular cheese can be very high in fat and sodium. Even cheese that is made up of fat-free or skim milk can contain a lot of sodium and fat, because, oftentimes, extra cream is added. The fat percentage of cheese is based off of the amount of water it contains. This means that the more water a certain type of cheese contains, the less percentage of fat it will have.

Fat-free or low-fat cheeses are much better for your health than regular cheese. For example, regular cheese contains about 5g of fat, 70 calories, and 10% calcium, while cheese that is made from 2% milk contains 3g of fat, 50 calories, and 15% calcium.

Who says dieting has to be boring? After all, you are allowed to have fun isn't that the way it's supposed to be?

Mix it up by trying different types of milk and dairy products. For example:

Cow's Milk

Whole milk from a cow contains about 8g of fat per 8fl oz (240-ml) serving and 150 calories. Fat-free milk contains 86 calories. Both contain Vitamin A and D.

Soy Milk

Soy milk is a good milk to use for people who are lactose intolerant. It does not contain casin. This type of milk contains 79% protein and 5g of fat. The good thing about soy is that it doesn't contain any cholesterol and has about 80 calories. The best choice of soy milk to buy would be fortified.

Almond Milk

Almond milk is very tasty and is another good choice of milk to choose for those who are lactose intolerant. It is also low in fat content and low in sugar, which is a plus.

Goat's Milk

Goat's milk is actually free of lactose, while not containing much fat at all. The best choices are the ones that are rich in Calcium and Vitamin D.

Oat Milk

Oat milk contains a little less lactose than cow's milk. However, this form of milk contains more vitamins, such as niacin, B3 and B6, calcium, copper, potassium, and selenium. The bad news is that oat milk contains more fat than all the other milk varieties and may be harder to find as a low-fat form.

SHEEP'S MILK

If you are looking for a type of milk with a content of rich protein, sheep milk would be your best bet, because it is rich in minerals and fats. However, sheep milk can be hard to come by and may have to be specially ordered or found in whole food stores.

THE CONTENT OF MILK

Whole milk contains 72% fat and 291mg calcium.

Lactose-reduced 2% milk contains 40% fat and 302-mg calcium.

Low-fat milk contains 27% fatmand 300mg calcium.

Butter milk contains 18% fat and 285mg calcium.

Fat-free milk contains 0% fat and 302mg of calcium.

Reduced-fat 2% milk contains 45% fat 297mg calcium.

Enriched soy milk contains about 35% fat and 240mg of calcium.

Although regular milk, fat-free, and low-fat milk content is just a few numbers of different, believe it or not, just by choosing milk that contains less fat and calories, it could make a very big difference in your daily diet and your health, especially when exercise is added to your regimen.

CHAPTER 11

THE STRENGTH IN SUPPLEMENTS

Some people are highly against the use of supplements and might even wish that there wasn't such a thing. However, there are a few good reasons on why supplements are good for the body. They can be used as substitutes for when certain foods don't contain the right amounts of vitamins and minerals the body needs. And also are good for helping to improve the body's health. Supplements can and may be found in varies forms such as capsules, gel caps, tablets, powders, and liquids.

Before buying any type of supplement, always consult a doctor or a nutritionist and always do your research. Some of the stock that are sold on the markets tend to vary in quality, especially because they can be manufactured by different companies and what that might mean is that they can add extra preservatives, which is something you want to stay clear of.

One of the reasons why supplements do exist is because the majority of foods that are consumed by us usually do not contain much vitamins and minerals at all, which can leave the body starved of what it needs for better health. Foods that have been overly processed or sometimes sitting in cans and on shelves for a long time are some of the major reasons on why this can occur.

There are many different manufacturing supplement companies that make these compounds for our body's needs, but they also make them differently for a reason: Is it perhaps so that they can set themselves apart from all the other existing companies? For example, not all creatine products are all made pure. Some may even contain sugar, just for the sake of the consumer and the buyer.

Supplements are not really a bad choice to make just as long as you know what you are putting into your body. They are also good for helping to improve the body's health and may even prevent diseases like cancer, osteoporosis, and cardio vascular disease.

The percentage of people in the U.S. that use supplements in their daily routine are between 28 and 40 percent. However, it is always important to keep in mind that since supplements have good benefits on helping to improve a person's health, it is also advised that anybody that takes them should do it with precautions. Never take more than the recommended dosage or for an excessive amount of time.

Supplements are not to be treated like medications, specifically because they do not get tested or monitored the way medications do before being sent out to be prescribed by people with sicknesses. However, when a certain supplement is being looked at by food and drug administration (FDA), they make sure to prevent the sale of whatever they have proof of not being safe to be for the public consumption.

A manufacturing supplement company will make general claims about how good their products are, but they can't keep back references to prevent or cure any type of disease.

Before buying any form of supplement make sure to do your homework on whatever it is your interested in buying, regardless of whether it is for putting on size, for getting ripped, or just for general health purposes. And avoid anything that might contain compounds, such as the herb ephedra.

OMEGA-3, 6, AND 9

Here are three types of fatty acids for promoting good health: Omega 3, 6, and 9. However, out of all, Omega 3 can help you accelerate fat burning. This is especially good if your goal is to lose weight. This can also regulate your appetite. It is also important to take these fatty acids.

Fish and flaxseed oil contains a lot of Omega—3. Omega—3 also contains alpha-linolenic acid. This helps reduce the storage of fat. Omega-3 fats play a very crucial role in burning fat. The best sources of Omega—3's come from cold water fish, such as salmon, sardines, herring, and mackerel.

It is best to consume at least seven to ten ounces of fish per week. However, if you prefer to get your Omega-3's from flaxseed instead of fish, then it's best to consume two to four tablespoons a day. But, the preferred dosage is four tablespoons a day along with each meal.

And even if you are not a big vegetable fan, I highly suggest eating them every day. You can also get your sources of Omega-3 from plant products as well. These are foods such as pumpkin seed, hempseed, grapeseed, flaxseed, kale, purslane, collard greens, and also parsley. These are all good because they all contain alpha-linoleic acid in their chloroplasts.

Flaxseed Oil

Flaxseed oil has a lot of good benefits. It also contains 27 identifiable, cancer-preventative compounds. Flaxseed is good for helping in the prevention of developing prostate and breast cancer. It can also help regulate blood sugar, blood pressure, and even lower bad cholesterol. If you take your regular dosage of flaxseed daily, it will increase your metabolic rate, give you much healthier skin, and keep you leaner than those who do not take it. Flaxseed oil is so good for you that it is said that it also enhances your immune system, helps with heart health, and even helps menopausal symptoms.

HOLY BASIL

This herb is also known as tulsi. Holy basil is a very beneficial supplement because it contains hundreds of photochemical that can help you. It is also very effective at regulating the body's response to stress, especially the cortisol response. This helps improve the fighting capacity of your body against a lot of stress.

During our everyday lives, we deal with a lot of stress. A few reasons for this may be caused by working excessively long hours at work, improper nutrition, and/or staying up late and not getting enough rest.

Cortisol is one of the stress hormones that increase blood sugar levels so that the body gets plenty of fuel. The blood sugars also acts as a type of fuel source. When the body experiences an excessive amount of stress, the cortisol and blood sugar just keeps adding up. Another reason for this is because the toxins that we consume, such as alcohol, coffee, cigarettes, and also processed foods.

Basil helps regulate cortisol when the body is experiencing stress and by normalizing the blood sugar levels. If you are overweight and your glucose levels are high, then your risk of developing diabetes could be high, since excess sugar is stored as fat.

Holy basil, or tulsi, may also help relieve anxiety and depression. It is said that drinking at least one cup a day could be beneficial, and drinking more will maximize your body's health.

Conjugated Linoleic Acid

Conjugated linoleic acid is a type of supplement that is used to help promote lean muscle tissue and fat loss. If you are struggling to lose that last extra amount of fat around your midsection area then this supplement is definitely effective in helping to do the job.

Conjugated linoleic acid can also help increase your metabolic rate by preventing lipid genesis and fat storage after a eating. CLA can be found in ground turkey, beef, cheese, and milk.

Although fats are not good for you, it is important to get some fats for health and to utilize your nutrients intake properly.

CLA also helps to enhance the immune system. The recommended dosage for this supplement should be 1-3g or 1000—3000mg.

Hoodia

Hoodoo is a type of fruit that comes from the cactus plant. This plant is also used by the san bush men of the Kalahari Desert. Because they are from a very harsh environment, they use the hoodoo fruit to quench their thirst and to stop themselves from getting hungry. This plant is very beneficial, because it also can be used as an appetite suppressant.

It is said that the most effective part of hoodoo comes from the actual core and stems. When taking this supplement it is best to at least take a dosage of 400 mg to 700mg.

Bee Pollen

Bee pollen can be very effective in many ways because it contains a lot of minerals, vitamins, proteins, Vitamins B1, B2, B3, B5, B6, B12, A, C, and E, and arytenoids, magnesium, copper, folic acidrutin, minerals, calcium, silica, sulfur, phosphorus, manganese, and chlorine enzymes.

Bee pollen has a wide range of amino acids and has a more concentrated source of protein. Bee pollen is very supportive of the nervous system and reproductive systems. Bee pollen also contains a type of protein that can be easily digested if taken on an empty stomach and readily accessible for use of the body. This is also good for lessening hunger too.

Bee pollen also has very powerful antioxidants which can help reduce the free radical damage from the bad toxins that we take in everyday.

Bee pollen is known for its high rutin levels. This is also found in many other types of plants, such as apple skins, green tea, and buckwheat as well. Rutin is good for strengthening the capillaries and can help improve the overall endurance of cardiovascular system. If you are ever feeling hungry, and you want to get rid of the hunger pains, then try taking one teaspoon at least a half hour before your first meal on an empty stomach.

Bee pollen is natural, and also contains necessary digestive enzymes, fatty acids, and a lot of phytonutrients. Some people may be allergic to bee pollen, so it is important that you consult a doctor and do as much research as you can to build some knowledge of any supplement before taking it.

Gamma—Oryzanol and Brown Rice

It is far better to eat brown rice instead of white rice, because of the difference in the nutritional value. For example, brown rice is not only healthier for you, but it contains less carbs and even tastes better too.

Unrefined brown rice can also reduce blood sugar levels, while white rice just does the opposite. This is also important for fighting off obesity and keeping unwanted weight off. Brown rice is always good to eat with a good dieting plan, especially with some mixed veggies. The grain that the brown rice is coated in is the most nutrient-rich and dense. It contains at least 70 antioxidants that can help you preserve your youthfulness and protect you from cellular damage.

The bran part of brown rice contains a type of Vitamin E that is known as tocotrienol, which helps the body in lowering cholesterol and cutting fat. Polysaccharides are also found in the bran part of the rice. This is very complex, especially suited for high blood sugar, obesity, and diabetes.

Gamma—oryzanol is also a potent antioxidant and can be purchased as an oil and taken by teaspoon once a day. This type of compound can help strengthen the muscles. Brown rice bran also contains a lot of coq10.

Human Growth Hormone—HGH

While you are sleeping, your body produces its own growth hormones, especially during your youth years.

Of course, you already know how important sleep is. Sleep is important because if the body doesn't get it then a drop in your natural production of HGH can occur. This means you won't have to go to the bathroom every so often or waking up for a midnight snack.

Sodium

Sodium or sodium chloride is found in table salt. Sodium is very important for controlling the water that the body contains, and it is good for maintaining proper pH or acidity and alkalinity of the blood that transmits nerve signals by helping the muscles to contract. All foods contain sodium. Even processed foods contain added sodium.

Sodium is sometimes over consumed. Meaning that a person consumes about twenty times the recommended daily requirements, which is 500mg. Of course, we all may already know this, but yet we still ignore the consequences of what can happen. A high intake of sodium can result in vomiting, abdominal cramps, diarrhea, and nausea. When the body loses excess amounts of fluid, it is caused by high concentrations of sodium, which can also be harmful and cause swelling, difficulty breathing, high blood pressure, and heart failure. Since our dietary intake of sodium is high, sodium deficiency is rare. However, it would be best to avoid having such complications, especially when trying to keep our sodium intake on a moderate level.

You don't want it to be low either, because this can cause heavy sweating and dehydration, which can occur to a person when involved in sports, running, and also during extremely hot weather. This could also be a problem to people that suffers from kidney disease. Sodium deficiency can also cause vomiting, muscle cramps, drowsiness, headache, fainting, and nausea. You could even slip into a coma, experience fatigue, and/or can be fatal.

COPPER

Copper acts as an antioxidant, which helps to maintain the myelin sheath. The myelin sheath is the part that surrounds and protects your nerve fibers and the functioning of the nerves system. Copper is also part of the processing of iron in the body and in the forming of red blood cells. Copper plays an important part in the functioning of the body, such as hair, eyes, and the production of skin pigment. It also helps in the development of healthy teeth, bones, and heart and protects your body's cells from chemical damage. The sources of foods that you can get copper from, such as whole grains, seafood (like lobster, crab, and oyster), sesame seeds, almonds, Brazil nuts, and pistachios. All the foods that I just mentioned contain at least 1mg per 1 3/4oz (50g) and contain natural sources of copper. Although copper plays an important role in the body, it can also have bad side effects, especially when left untreated.

Although rare, it has been known to occur to infants that are malnourished. It could also cause excessive bleeding, which is caused by reduced production of red blood cells and damage to the connecting tissue. It is safe to say that the requiring daily dosage is 0.9 mg per day.

CALCIUM

Calcium is a main mineral that is present in both your teeth and bones. This is where 99% of the body's calcium is contained.

And the remaining percent is used by the body's functions for nerve signals, muscle contractions, and blood clotting.

When the calcium is absorbed in the intestine, it is also regulated by Vitamin D. Lactose can also help to enhance the absorption of calcium, which is sugar that is found in the dairy products, phytate, and oxalate and are also contained in parsley, celery, spinach, and beets. These vegetables can help cut the body's ability to absorb calcium.

If you are on a high protein diet, you would be passing more when you urinate. This is why people who have kidney stones are advised to reduce their protein intake.

Children between the ages of 7 to 18 years of age actually need to take more calcium then children who are younger and young adults in order to promote the development of healthy strong bones and there growth. As of right now, there isn't any deficiency of calcium and probably won't be for a while. Because the bones still release calcium into the blood to keep it normal for just in case the mineral intake is low.

Signs of calcium deficiency are bone pain, sharp needle like pains in your hands or feet, twitching, osteoporosis, muscle cramps, and convulsions. These are caused by the weakening of the bones that can lead to them fracture and eventually crumble. This also leads to a loss of height. This is why it was very important for you to get in as much calcium as possible when you were younger and still important now. Trust me, I have my own child, and as a father, I make sure she gets her daily intake of calcium by drinking a lot of milk so that she can grow to be strong, beautiful, and healthy.

When a person doesn't get enough calcium during childhood, they will end up increasing their chances of developing osteoporosis when they get older. This also stunts their growth, causes muscle cramps, twitching, muscle weakening, and irritability if left untreated the calcium deficiency in a child's life can be fatal.

The best sources to make sure that you are getting plenty of calcium are turnip greens, collard greens, canned salmon, spinach, bok choy, dairy products, mustard greens, tofu, almonds, and sardines. All of these foods contain at least 150 mg of calcium per 3 ½ oz (100g). Don't forget if you are a parent, a daily intake of these foods are also good for your child as well.

MAGNESIUM

Magnesium is a mineral that helps with the formation of teeth and bones. Also helps with the absorption of minerals like sodium, potassium, and calcium, which transmit nerve signals and cause muscle contractions. Magnesium also plays a vital role and helping to process fat and protein. It is also necessary for the secretion for a hormone called parathyroid hormone.

Parathyroid hormone helps control calcium levels in the blood. The increase and absorption of potassium in the intestine is caused by Vitamin D. When it is absorbed, magnesium is then stored in the muscles, cells, fluid, and the bone that holds up the body. Some doctors use magnesium to reduce irregular heart rhythms and for some pregnant women during contractions. If the intake of magnesium is too high, it can result in giving intestinal problems and cause bad absorption of nutrients, kidney disease, hyperparathyroidism, excessive vomiting, alcohol abuse, long time use of medications, and liver cirrhosis.

Magnesium is also needed for the normal functioning of a gland called parathyroid gland. When the gland secretes the parathyroid hormone, low magnesium levels end up decreasing the levels of calcium in the blood. The deficiency of magnesium can also lead to low levels of calcium and potassium in the blood and change the digestive system, muscular system, nervous system, circulatory system, and the crucial development of the blood cells. This also causes poor appetite, anemia, fatigue, impaired speech, irregular heart rhythms, and body tremors. If not treated, it could be fatal.

The proper dosage of magnesium is 420 mg per a daily requirement. Natural sources of magnesium can be found in okra, lamb kidney, swiss chard, red meat, spinach, whole grains, legumes, artichokes, almonds, tofu, Brazil nuts, peanuts, cashews, and sunflower seeds. Each of these natural foods contain at least 50 mg of magnesium per 3 ½ oz (100g).

Phosphorus

Phosphorus is found in fats and fat-like compounds, such as carbohydrates, protein, enzymes, and DNA that our genes are made of. Phosphorus is also important for the teeth and bones. It is also found in a compound called adenosine triphosphate, otherwise known as ATD. This is stored as energy that is needed by the cells.

Vitamin D is also an important compound for the absorption of phosphorus. Although phosphorus is essential for your teeth and bones, taking an excessive amount of antacid indigestion medication for a long period of time may cause a phosphorus deficiency. Additionally, if you combine antacids with phosphorus, it will prevent the absorption into the blood stream. This will also cause bone pain and muscle weakness. You can even experience abnormal secretion of calcium in the urine, anemia, and nervous system problems, kidney stones, and some psychological disorders. The best way to avoid these complications are to take phosphorus in a moderate dosage of 700-mg per day.

Potassium

Potassium chloride and sodium all share the same responsibility of controlling the amount of water and also helps to maintain the correct acid alkali balance in the body. Potassium is essential for helping the body store sugar in the form of glycogen. This is a source of energy that the muscles need in order to work properly. Potassium is also important for the functioning of the kidneys, heart, heart valves, muscles, adrenal glands, and the nerve cells.

A regular intake of natural foods with high potassium can actually help lower and control blood pressure. This is also important for people with high blood pressure or heart failure to eat a good amount of this mineral.

There are good sources of food that you can get potassium from. These include bananas, avocados, tomatoes, oranges, red meat, spinach, whole grains, asparagus, cantaloupe, lima beans, dairy products, and especially potatoes. Potatoes are high in potassium and contain a good source of folate, protein, fiber, and iron. Potatoes are also much healthier for you when baked or boiled instead of fried. Which means going to a fast food gig and ordering a value meal with a side of French fries would be out of the question. All of the foods that I had just mentioned contain at least 160mg of potassium per 3 ½ oz (100g).

A high intake in calcium can also help decrease your chances of developing kidney stones, stroke, and osteoporosis. It is also important to eat a great variety of foods that are high in potassium during warm weather, because you lose a great amount of it thru your body when you sweat. You also want to avoid having a low level of potassium in the blood. This is known as hypokalemia and is caused by the loss of this mineral. Loss of potassium could also result in developing kidney disease, diarrhea, metabolic disorder, and vomiting.

But the good news about taking potassium is that it isn't bad for you when your intake is of moderate dosage and combined with a proper diet your daily potassium intake should be 3,500 mg per day.

IRON

Iron is an important mineral that is found in all cells that the body contains. Although iron is needed in very small quantities, it is known as a component of hemoglobin, which is oxygen that carries protein in red blood cells and also carry the oxygen around the body, which is also part of myoglobin. Myoglobin is a type of protein that is found in the muscle cells and helps release energy from glucose and fatty acids in the intestine. The absorption of iron requires gastric acid which is secreted by a lining of the stomach to turn it into a form that is better absorbed.

Heme iron is a type of iron that comes from animal meat, and it is easier for the body to absorb then the iron found in plants. When Vitamin C is present in the body, it increases the absorption of iron from plant foods. When the need for iron is really needed by the body, it absorbs a great amount of it from the food that you consume.

This is especially important for women who are pregnant or who have might of lost a lot of blood after child birth, heavy menstrual cycle, people with anemia, trauma, and/or people who have gone through surgery. The best way for good recovery from a whole lot of blood loss is to get a good amount of iron from foods, such as spinach, because it contains a good source of iron and also contain Vitamins C, E, calcium, folate, beta carotene, and potassium. Iron can also be found in other foods, such as egg yolks, animal kidney, chick peas, kidney beans, liver, lima beans, poultry, red meat, sardines, prunes, shrimp, and soy. These are all natural foods that contain a good source of iron and at least contain 2-mg of iron, 3 ½ oz (100g) each.

However, a poor intake of iron is usually caused by changes in the body's metabolic rate, which sometimes occurs to new mothers, women during menstruating, children and infants, women who breastfeed, pregnant women, and older adults. Also when a baby isn't breast fed and not given formula that contains iron, it may also develop what is known as iron deficiency.

People who eat more meat actually get more iron than those who are vegetarians. Since vegetarians only eat plant-based foods, their bodies contain less iron, because vegetables don't have as much iron as meat does. This makes a vegetarian more vulnerable to iron deficiency. A daily amount of iron should at least be 8-mg per day for men. And the intake for women should be 18-mg, since a women's body can go through more than a man's, especially with their ability to give birth, breastfeed, and for the fact that they go through periods of times when they have their menstrual cycles.

IODINE

Iodine is found in all of the body's cells and 40 percent of it is stored in the thyroid gland. Iodine is used in the thyroid gland for making thyroid hormones. This is important for the growth of a normal body and metabolism. Iodine is a natural source that is already contained in the sea, which means whenever we eat seafood or any type of sea plant grown in the sea or near it that would be the way of us getting our natural source of iodine intake.

A majority of the table salt sold at local supermarkets and what we have at our homes contain iodine. When we urinate, we tend to get rid of the excess amounts of what we get in our diets. Although an excessive amount of iodine wouldn't be considered to be healthy, it is still an important mineral that the body needs in order to function right. When the body doesn't get enough iodine, the production in thyroid hormones decreases and grow larger.

Swelling in the neck could also occur as well as cretinism, dwarfism, and cause difficulties learning. These symptoms are also caused by what is known as goiter. This usually occurs to people that do not get enough salt in their diets and also to those who live in parts of the world where iodine isn't easy to come by. The proper requiring intake for iodine should be at least 0.15 mg per day.

Although just about any food tastes good when a little salt is added, it is still best to be very careful not to go on a salt overdose.

Sulfur

Sulfur is important in converting carbohydrates to a form that the body can use, and also helps manufacture the amino acids. Sulfur is used in insulin, which is a hormone in the body that is secreted by the pancreas. The pancreas helps regulate the levels of sugar/glucose in the blood. It also helps make connective tissue that surrounds the body structures and also holds them together, such as nails, skin, and hair and also helps manufacture vitamins biotin, thiamine, and B1 in the body. Since sulfur deficiency occurs naturally in foods, it has not been diagnosed in anybody yet. However, there are still plenty of natural sources of foods to get sulfur from. And each of these foods contain at least 100mg of sulfur per 3 1/ 2 oz (100-mg), such as bean sprouts, cabbage, chicken, dairy products, egg yolks, kale, legumes, nuts, organ meats, raspberries, red meat, sea food, and turnip greens.

The daily requirement of sulfur should at least range from 800-1,000-mg per day. Honestly, out of all 13 food choices that I had just mentioned, my favorite choice would be raspberries, because they are a good source of fiber and contain magnesium, iron, Vitamin C, and calcium, and they also taste good, too.

Raspberries make the perfect fruit to just sit back and enjoy, either by themselves, mixed with other fruits, in a fruit smoothie, or even with a small bowl of fat-free vanilla ice cream and, of course, almonds.

I know that I may sound like I am getting a little carried away, but that is just the way I get when I talk about food of any sort. Ice cream can make a very tasty treat as long as it's fat-free and eaten at a moderate proportion.

CHROMIUM

Chromium is a micro-mineral that helps insulin in the body get together with the receptors on the membrane in the cells in the body. By working with insulin, chromium also helps it regulate the levels of sugar glucose by letting it move into the cells, where it once produced energy that the body's cells need. Chromium is very essential for the body, and when combined together with insulin, they play an important part in the body's functioning. Without the body's intake of chromium, a deficiency could occur, especially in people who have to rely on long-term use of feeding through the vein because of the lack of poor nutrition, or marathon runners who run long distance cross country races. Marathon runners tend to lose a good amount of it through their urine, especially when they increase their endurance.

The best way to make up for chromium loss is by making sure that you are getting plenty of it through a clean, healthy diet. The proper daily intake should be at least 0.035 mg. Natural sources of chromium can also be found in apples, which provides an excellent source of fiber, quercetin, and flavornoid phytochemical. Flavornoid phytochemical also helps lower blood cholesterol.

Chromium can also be found in bananas, beef, broccoli, green beans, grapes, ham, oranges, potatoes, pork, red meat, tomatoes, and turkey. By choosing to eat from a great variety of these foods, you will be getting a minimum of 1mg per 1 3/ 4 oz (50g) each.

FLUORIDE

Fluoride is a mineral that can be found in water or sometimes added when the source is of poor quality. Fluoride is often added to soil to help grow plants and vegetables. Small amounts of fluoride are also present in the body, which 99 percent of it is present in your bones and teeth. Fluoride is also very important for being able to increase the minerals that are in your teeth and density in your bones, and it can also help reduce the risk of developing diseases, such as tooth decay.

Fluoride also helps promote the mineral of the enamel throughout your life as well. Fluoride is very beneficial for your health, because, without it, you would be more likely to suffer from other bad health that could also lead to heart problems. However, not everyone in the United States is considered to be very lucky. Some of them tend to live in poor communities and are usually the ones who don't have access to alternative fluoride resources. Because of these problems, children are more likely to get really sick and develop further health complications. This is known as a deficiency. Which can cause slow metabolism and unwanted, excess weight gain. This isn't good for young children, because it can also give them problems, like learning disabilities and reduced growth of the muscles and skeleton.

A daily requirement for fluoride intake should at least be 4 mg per day.

Why Supplements Can Be Helpful

Generally, a multivitamin can be able to provide some extra nutrition for the body, just in case you happen to not be getting the proper nutrition you need, due to the type of food you might be consuming. Multivitamins can also be beneficial for women who are pregnant.

There has been some question of whether or not Vitamin E is effective in helping to treat cardiovascular disease. Although, there has been a clinical study for over 30 years on what the effects of Vitamin E were for, preventing certain people from developing cardiovascular disease would depend on who would be at risk or not. Vitamin E was proven to be ineffective in some recent trials on developing cardiovascular disease.

However, chromium is very important to the body for helping to process insulin and also for controlling the glucose in the blood. Keep in mind that supplements cannot prevent people who are at risk of diabetes or prevent them from getting it.

WHEN TO LIMIT SUPPLEMENTS

It is always best to keep in mind that supplements are not medication, and the results of harmful effects are caused by taking too much vitamins and minerals, which is a definite no, no on excessive intake of supplementing. The only time that you might be able to take extra dosages of supplements is if you were to be advised by your doctor while being monitored.

The type of vitamins that can be stored in the liver are Vitamins A, D, E, and even K. By taking an excessive amounts of these vitamins, a buildup may occur much faster than those of water soluble vitamins, such as Vitamins B and C. However, there are a lot of vitamins that can be harmful when taken in large amounts.

For example, taking an excessive amount of Vitamin A can cause headaches, lips to crack, dried skin, and even blurred vision.

Taking too much Vitamin C can give you diarrhea and kidney stones.

Taking Vitamin D in excessive amounts can lead to vomiting, loss of appetite, calcium deposits in the body tissues, and also cause nausea.

Taking too much Vitamin B-Complex can cause flushing, light headedness, itching, tingling, improper balance in the legs, and nausea.

The good news about these symptoms are that they do not last long.

Overall, the pros of supplements far outweigh the cons. However, it is always best to get your vitamins and minerals from all natural, whole foods.

Chapter 12

The Might in Minerals

Minerals are a substance that is originated from rocks and ores. Many minerals are important for health. We get them by eating plants, which get their minerals from the soil, or by eating animals that have eaten the plants. And also by drinking water that contains minerals. Minerals are very important for the body, and they are needed in tiny quantities, which are called macro-minerals or micro-minerals, depending to what the percentage of your total body weight they constitute and how much you need to consume in your daily diet.

Macro-minerals are made up of more than 0.005 percent of your body's weight, and you would need to be taking at least more than 10 mg of these daily. These should include phosphorus, calcium, sodium, magnesium, potassium, and sulfur.

Micro-minerals are also known as trace elements. They make up less than 0.005 percent of your body's weight, and you would need less than 100mg daily. Micro-minerals that have identified roles in health are iodine, selenium, chromium, fluoride, iron, zinc, and copper.

WHY MINERALS ARE NEEDED

Minerals work by making and helping to break down body tissues and helping to regulate metabolism and the chemical reactions that constantly occur in our body. For example, our bones consist of a type of protein collagen, which most of the body's phosphorus, calcium, and magnesium are deposited. Your bones contain minerals that are stored so that if your diet was poor, such as a calcium deficiency, the bones can release some of the minerals for the body's needs. The teeth also contain minerals, phosphorus, and calcium.

Minerals can be found in many key molecules in the body, and they are also involved in essential chemical reactions, such as sulfur. Sulfur is a part of Thiamine (B1).: Calcium activates a digestive enzyme that breaks down fats. While copper is needed to incorporate iron into hemoglobin, the oxygen-carrying molecule that is present in red blood cells. Calcium, magnesium, and sodium are very important in cell functioning, especially in the transmission of electrical impulses along nerve fibers and in muscle contractions.

Minerals are also in most foods in varying quantities. Red meat also has a good source of iron that is need by the body to make red blood cells.

Mineral Deficiencies

The most wide spread mineral deficiencies in North America and diseases that they cause are caused by iron. Iron deficiencies include enlarged thyroid glands, loss of calcium, lack of iodine, anemia, osteoporosis, tooth decay, and fluoride. Because of the fact that the body stores and reuses minerals, it may be a while before people start getting symptoms. The reason for mineral deficiency is because of a primary or secondary deficiency.

Primary deficiency will occur if you are not getting enough of minerals in your diet. And secondary deficiency occurs when your diet is adequate, but another factor results in the body when it can't absorb or use a mineral. When a mineral is poorly absorbed, it is usually caused by a disorder of the intestine, such as a disease called Crohn's disease, which can be caused by the intake of too many medications or other substances that are in the food connected to minerals and prevent them from being absorbed. The consumption of too much alcohol, sweating and medication intake can also be the reason for the loss of minerals from the body.

How to Get Enough Minerals

There is no single food out there that is considered to be the best source of minerals. However, eating a good variety of foods will ensure that you get enough and also the body can be able to store minerals for future use, especially when your intake of minerals are low. Meats from animals are the best source of minerals, because they contain proportions of minerals that are just right for our bodies. Vegetables and fruits are also good sources, especially if they are organic. Any type of vegetable or fruit that is organically grown contains more minerals than those that are grown non-organically.

Mineral water is a source of minerals that includes magnesium.

When a food is processed the minerals are often lost. For example, chromium, iron, and potassium are removed from whole grains, while going thru the refining process. The law states that when a certain mineral is lost during processing that it must be replaced. Enriched grains are refined and contain added iron to compensate for the amounts that are lost. The nutrients that are lost are often not replenished. Some table salt contains iodine that is added to it. All milk and breakfast cereals are fortified with a variety of minerals that are essential for promoting good health.

Minerals are different from vitamins, because they do not get damaged by light or heat. However, some minerals can be lost in the water that is used for cooking. It is best to try to avoid boiling vegetables so that you can preserve the minerals that they contain. Instead, try steaming them by using as little water as possible or keeping the cooking time short by using the microwave method. If you are one who likes to boil your vegetables, then you can also put them in the water while the water is already at a boiling point because putting the vegetables in cold water and then boiling them will only result in many more lost nutrients.

If you are still not getting the right amount of minerals that your body requires, then try taking them in supplement form.

CHAPTER 13

THE VALUE OF VITAMINS

Vitamins play an important role in the proper functioning of the body. They can also be obtained by either supplemental form or in natural form, such as food, fruits and vegetables. Without vitamins, people would not be able to live a healthy life and would always be sick.

It is crucial to consume foods that are rich in antioxidants, because they can benefit the health. Consider antioxidants to be the good guys and free radicals as its enemy. Antioxidants help to take down free radicals from the body. If free radicals build up, they will damage the body's cells and tissues and later lead to disease. A diet high in fruits and vegetables reduces the risk of developing diseases and cancers.

VITAMIN DEFICIENCIES

Vitamin deficiency can either be two things, one of them is primary and the other one is secondary. The cause of primary deficiency is when you don't get enough of vitamins from what you consume. A secondary deficiency can happen if you are an avid smoker, an excessive alcohol consumer, or if you take medication for a long time. These factors will interfere with the absorption of vitamins that the body relies on for its use. Vitamin deficiency also causes diseases known as pellagra (niacin deficiency), beriberi (thiamine deficiency), scurvy (Vitamin C deficiency), and rickets (Vitamin D deficiency).

Today, in the United States, deficiencies are rare, because the plentiful food supplies and thanks to the healthy food programs that are available. People without the proper materials to afford such foods do not have to worry. In addition, programs do add vitamins and minerals to a majority of foods.

VITAMINS AND WHAT THEY DO

Vitamins are very essential for the body, because they help by promoting the health of the immune system, hormonal system, and the nervous system. Vitamins can either be obtained from foods, such as fruits and vegetables, or by supplements. This is very crucial because our bodies are not able to make vitamins on their own. There are 13 vitamins total. These vitamins are known as Vitamin C and Vitamin B-Complex, water soluble or fat soluble, Vitamin A, D, E, and K.

Lets first start off with the fat soluble vitamins. For instance, fat soluble vitamins are the type of vitamins that can be absorbed with fat from the intestine and then circulated through the body. After they have been absorbed into the circulation of the body, they are then carried to the liver to be stored. This process is very important, because if the body were to ever experience any disorder or disease, it could affect the absorption of fat, such as celiac disease, which is one of the causes that could also lead to a vitamin deficiency.

The vitamins that make up of fat soluble are Vitamins A, D, E, and K. These are the type of vitamins that the liver is able to store. While the body is able to store vitamins such as these, Vitamin E can also be distributed through the body's fatty tissues. Now, let's talk about water soluble vitamins.

Water soluble vitamins are the types that include Vitamins C and B. these two types of vitamins can only be stored in the body for a short period of time, but then go on to be excreted by the kidneys. The only vitamin that is stored by the liver is Vitamin B12. Water soluble vitamins are very important for the body's overall health and also crucial that the average person always includes them into their diets as well.

Vitamins, such as the B-Complex group and Vitamin C, ascorbic acid, are made up of at least nine water soluble vitamins. Vitamin B-Complex makes up of a total of 8 group vitamins.

Here is a look at each vitamin and what role that they play in the different parts of the body, what happens when the body receives too much or too little, how they can be obtained, and the requirement intake of vitamins and minerals.

Vitamin A

Vitamin A plays a special role in helping to promote vision, such as night vision, healthy skin, normal bone growth, reproduction, and mucous membranes. The mucous membrane is the layer part that secretes mucous and lines the body regions, such as the respiratory tract.

Vitamin A acts as an antioxidant in the body and also protects the body by reducing its chances of developing cancers. There are two forms of Vitamin A sources. One of these forms comes from animals, which is known as retinoids. Retinoids include retinol and retinal. And the other form is known as precursors or pro vitamins. These can be converted to an active form by the body.

When choosing the proper intake of vitamins, you either have the choice of getting it from supplementing by pill form, liquid, powder, or food form. I always choose to get my daily intake of vitamins from food sources. These foods include fruits and vegetables. I try to pick the ones that are dark colors, like orange, yellow, and also of green pigmentation. Fruits and vegetables that contain these colors are called carotenoids.

Certain amounts of vitamins are measured in equivalents, usually written as R.E. One R.E. of beta carotene is equivalent to 0.001mg of retinal or 0.006mg or 3.3 international units.

When a person takes Vitamin A, their body takes it and allows the vitamin to make its way to the intestine. Once the vitamin gets to the intestine, the intestine then has a job to protect the vitamin by keeping it from being changed by chemicals that are given off by Vitamin E. Vitamin A can also be stored in the body, because it is fat soluble.

In order to make sure that your vitamin intake is on point, you would at least need to eat a lot of fruits and vegetables. Yes, I know that by me saying this it sounds funny, especially having to remind a whole bunch of young adults and older adults alike. But, trust me when I say this, fruits and vegetables really are good for you, and they can really benefit the body's needs and help promote good health. Who knows? Maybe by you choosing to eat healthier, you may live a little longer. And, of course, you can't forget to drink plenty of water and get the exercise that the body requires. This is a must.

Vitamin A is definitely one of the major key sources of vitamins that the body needs for promoting and maintaining the body's overall health. After the body receives the right amount of vitamins that it needs, the liver then releases some of the vitamin, which is carried by the blood and then delivered to the tissue and cells. The recommending dosage of this vitamin should be 900 R.E. per day. Although some people never really seem to have much problems taking care of themselves, getting plenty of exercise, and getting in their daily vitamins, others do. This may be because of the lack of resources or maybe the type of diet or lifestyle that they choose doesn't allow them to get the proper intake of vitamins that the body requires. Usually when the body doesn't meet its requirement of vitamin intake, it goes through a stage of deficiency. This happens when the body doesn't get enough vitamins, mainly because food resources are low and/or the country that they live in is underdeveloped. This is also common among people who consume a lot of alcohol, to newborns, and pregnant women.

Vitamin A deficiency can also affect people with long term conditions that enable them to absorb fats, such as cystic fibrosis or Crohn's disease. This also causes symptoms, such as an eye disorder known as xerophthalmia, which affects the transparent membrane at the front of the eye. This part of the eye is known as the cornea. Not only is the cornea affected, but it also makes it hard for the person to see at night. Xerophthalmia also leads to irreversible blindness and corneal ulceration.

Not only can this disease affect adults, but it can also affects children as well. These problems include rashes, such as follicular hyperkeratosis, troubles healing wounds, growth problems, dry bumpy skin, and the proper functioning of mucous membranes throughout the body.

Do you remember me mentioning that Vitamin A could also be obtained by eating fruits and vegetables? Well, here are 11 food examples from which you can get Vitamin A: apricots, cantaloupe, carrots, collard greens, kale, mango, pumpkin, spinach, sweet peppers, sweet potatoes and winter squash.

Each food source mentioned above contains at least 0.15 mg of Vitamin A per 1 ¾-7 oz (50-200g) serving.

Vitamin B

Vitamin B is made up of a group of eight individual vitamins known as B-Complex vitamins. These include the following:

B1—thiamine
B2—riboflavin
B3—niacin
B5—pantothenic acid
B6—pyridoxine b6
B7—biotin
B9—folic Acid
B12—cynocobalmin

These are all very important for helping the body break down carbohydrates and turning it into glucose, which then is used as energy for the body. Vitamin B also helps the body breakdown proteins and fats, which are used for the normal functioning of the nervous system, eyes, hair, liver, mouth, skin, and muscle tone in the stomach and intestinal tract.

Vitamin B-Complex is a vitamin that can be taken as a group supplement for overall good health. The cool thing about each of these vitamins is that they all have their special different functioning in the body. It important it is to get your daily intake of vitamins. You can choose the supplemental form, but nothing beats getting them the natural way from healthy food sources. These include the following: Brewer's yeast, eggs, fish, legumes, meats, milk, peanuts, and potatoes.

The recommended dosage of Vitamin B should be at least 920-2300 milligrams per day, depending on which complex of Vitamin B your body requires. Remember, they all have their job to do for different parts of the body's functioning, so the dosage may not be the same for each vitamin.

The reason why I would recommend, and rather, get my source of vitamins from food instead of just through supplements is because your chances on developing a certain deficiency are much slimmer than if you were to depend on reaching your daily intake requirements from supplementing. By eating a lot of fruits and vegetables, you're sure to be getting in pure vitamins and not added preservatives. Any deficiency can be bad for your health or even life threatening if not detected early and treated.

Vitamin B deficiency can cause the following: skin disorders, poor coordination, insomnia, disruption of the nervous system, ulcers, diarrhea, flushing tingling, nausea, skin eruptions, headaches, irritability, rapid pulse, muscle weakness, cramps, and may also cause pellagra.

Here is a look at what each form of Vitamin B does.

Vitamin B1 (thiamin) is essential for helping the body produce energy and also affects the enzymes that control the muscles, nerves, and heart.

Vitamin B2 (riboflavin) also shares the same responsibilities that B1 has.

Vitamin B3 (niacin) is important for helping to produce energy in the cells while maintaining healthy skin, a healthy digestive system, and nervous system.

Vitamin B5 (pantothenic acid) helps with the body's normal growth and development.

Vitamin B6 (pyridoxine) is important for helping the body to maintain overall health of the immune system, red blood cells, and break down proteins.

Vitamin B7 (biotin) is important for helping the body break down the carbohydrates and protein that it receives and by also helping the body to make hormones.

Vitamin B9 (folic acid) is very important in helping the body produce red blood cells and also helps the body make and maintain DNA.

Vitamin B12 (cynocobalmin) is important in helping the body grow and develop properly, and it is also able to help the body produce blood cells, the way the body uses carbohydrates and folic acid, and the functioning of the body's nervous system.

Vitamin C

Vitamin C plays an important role in helping the body fight off infections and colds. This vitamin has always been one of the top choices for decades, because of its ability to not only cure colds but to prevent them as well.

Vitamin C can also reduce histamire levels that are in the body. This is why it is important to try fitting this vitamin into you daily diet.

Just like every other vitamin source, getting an adequate amount and eating healthy is very crucial for the body's overall health.

Vitamin C is also important for forming collagen, which is a structural protein that is needed to strengthen bones and blood vessels. It also anchors your teeth into your gums. Vitamin C is also essential for the repair of tissue and the healing of wounds. This vitamin also acts like an antioxidant by protecting the body against infections and helping the white blood cells to break down nasty bacteria. It is also involved in producing red blood cells and the oxygen that they carry with the pigment hemoglobin by helping the body absorb iron from the intestine. Vitamin C it helps to treat and/or cure people who suffer from tuberculosis, fevers, surgery, burns, rheumatic arthritis, and pneumonia.

People with the above symptoms or health issues would obviously need more Vitamin C in their system to help them heal better. However, a regular person who would only be looking to stay healthy and avoid such infectious diseases and sicknesses should only take less than 500-mg per day. Because of the bad effects an excessive amount of Vitamin C can cause, it would be best to avoid taking excessive dosages. Too much Vitamin C could cause an upset stomach or even diarrhea. Doing so, may cause a deficiency by making the muscles weak, causing pain in the joints, loss of teeth, swollen gums, problems healing wounds, depression, fatigue, bruised skin or cause spots to appear on the skin, bleeding gums, rough, dry, scaly skin, dry, splitting hair, gingivitis, weak teeth enamel, pain in the joints, anemia, less ability to fight infections, and also slow down the metabolism.

A severe Vitamin C deficiency is known as scurvy, which can affect older adults, especially if they are malnourished.

Since Vitamin C isn't fat soluble, you should not consume a great amount of it every day. Also, it cannot be stored for use later on for the body's needs. Please keep in mind that everyone's recommended dosage may differ. This may not affect people who do not get enough Vitamin C in their diets, even those who are just following a strict diet.

When dieting, they are still at risk of getting sick, mainly because of the little amounts of fat that the body has. Drinkers and smokers are even at a greater risk of developing this deficiency, because it prevents their body's ability to absorb vitamins and other healthy minerals that are consumed by depleting their vitamin levels. They may require more Vitamin C than an average person who doesn't drink alcohol or smoke. If you happen to be in the category of either a smoker or a drinker, it would be best to talk to your doctor to see what would be best for you.

If you want to make a better change in your life by taking up a healthier lifestyle, then here are 16 food sources from which you can get Vitamin C: asparagus, bell peppers, broccoli, Brussels sprouts, cabbage, grapefruit, guava, kiwi, mango, melon, oranges, pineapples, plantain, strawberries, tomatoes, green peppers, turnip greens, sweet potatoes, white potatoes, tomatoes, cauliflower, cabbage winter squash, red peppers, straw berries, oranges, cantaloupe, mango, papaya, water melon, raspberries, pineapple, cranberries, blueberries and blackberries.

Each of the above mentioned foods contain at least 10mg of Vitamin C per 1 ¾-7 oz 950-200g) serving.

Vitamin D

Vitamin D plays an important role in absorbing and using phosphorus and calcium. It is also essential for keeping your bones, teeth, and cartilage (the fibrous part of the tissue that covers ends of your bones and joints) healthy.

There are two forms of Vitamin D—Vitamin D2 and Vitamin D3. These two vitamins are synthesized by the skin when exposed under sunlight. The body converts Vitamin D2 and Vitamin D3 into a form that it can use for healthy kidney and liver functioning. When the body senses that the levels of calcium in the blood are low, it releases a hormone from the neck called the parathyroid hormone, which comes from the parathyroid glands. This type of hormone helps stimulate the kidneys, making them turn the Vitamin D into an active form, which also stimulates the intestines by making it increase the absorption of phosphorus and calcium.

Vitamin D is can be found in dairy products, so developing a deficiency would almost be considered rare. However, people of and older age and those who are not able to get out into the sunlight much are more easily at risk to develop Vitamin D deficiency. Those who live in cold climates or people living in polluted urban areas are also at risk for a Vitamin D deficiency because of the lack of sunlight that they receive.

A good way to avoid Vitamin D deficiency is to avoid long time use of medications. These may interfere with turning Vitamin D into the active form. Even people with certain types of kidney diseases can end up being at risk of developing a deficiency, especially if their kidneys can't turn the Vitamin D into an active form that it is required to do.

Vitamin D deficiency causes the bones to soften, which is known as a disease called osteomalacia when adults have it. However, if it's a child that has it, it would be called rickets. Osteomalacia can also cause pain in the hips, muscles, legs, ribs. It makes your bones weak and more prone to injuries and breakage. Someone with a problem like this can even experience having trouble climbing stairs or sitting upright. This also deforms the bones, causing the person to be bowlegged and experience curvature of the spine.

However, there is hope! Many natural sources of foods contain Vitamin D. These include the following: dairy products, like milk, yogurt, and cheese, salmon, tuna, egg yolk, mackerel, halibut, liver oils, cod, and sardines.

Eating a great variety of these foods not only tastes good, but it also help promotes good health, ensuring you to live a happy, normal life.

The above mentioned varieties contain amounts of up to 0.003 mg of Vitamin D per 1 ¾-3 ½ oz (50-100g) serving.

If you are not getting this vitamin from any of these natural sources, then taking them in supplement form will contain at least 0.005 mg per day.

Vitamin E

Vitamin E is actually considered to be one of the most effective sources of vitamin out of all the vitamins. It's role is to help protect the body against free radicals as well as teaming up with Vitamin A and protecting it from becoming chemically changed. Not only do free radicals damage cells, they also cause the development of cardiovascular disease and cancer.

Vitamin E also helps the body make red blood cells and prevent the blood from clotting. Vitamin E is a fat soluble antioxidant that is able to stop the production of ROS from when the fats go through a state of oxidation. This vitamin is also one of the collective names of a group of fat soluble compounds with different antioxidant activities.

Vitamin E is stored in the muscle tissue, fat, and in the liver. This vitamin exists in eight different forms known as isomers—four tocopherols and four tocotrienols. These two are distinguished by the saturation of the side chain. The side chain of the four tocopherols is saturated, and the four tocotrienols side chains also contain three double bonds. These double bonds are connected with the methyl groups that are on the chromanol ring. The alpha form has at least three methyl groups. The beta and the gamma forms have only two methyl groups, while delta form has just one.

Each of these has its own biological activity. Alpha tocopherol is known for being the most effective biological antioxidant.

Tocotrienols have more antioxidants and are more potent than tocopherols. However, we can only digest tocotrienols poorly and eliminate it from the body rapidly. Tocotrienols can be absorbed by the skin and also used in creams.

Vitamin E is also used as a moisturizer, antioxidant, and a way to improve the skin in cosmetic care products, hair care products, and sunscreen agents. Although Vitamin E is one of the most effective sources of vitamins that the body needs, it would still be best to take it in a dosage of at least 0.015mg per day.

If a deficiency were to occur, chances are that it would only happen to people that have long-term problems that prevent them from absorbing fats from the intestine. This is a disease that is known as Crohn's disease and also in a disease that is known as cystic fibrosis. These signs also include problems with the nervous system and can cause anemia. This is caused by the short life span of the red blood cells.

However, you can never go wrong with the intake of Vitamin E from natural food sources if you choose not to get it from supplementing. These healthy food sources of Vitamin E include the following: almonds, hazelnuts, peanuts, pistachios, shrimp, soybeans, sun flower seeds, and wheat germ.

You would be getting at least 0.5mg of Vitamin E per 1-2 oz (28-55g) serving.

Vitamin K

Vitamin K is an essential component for the body's blood clotting process. This vitamin can also be found in healthy foods, such as fruits and vegetables. But the majority of it that we need is made by the gut known as the gut flora. These are small microorganisms that live naturally in the intestine, while the other remaining amount of it is stored in the liver.

When taking Vitamin K as an additional supplement, it is always best to be very careful, especially if you are already taking medications prescribed by your doctor. Just like most supplements, taking Vitamin K along with any type of medication will or may interfere with each other, depending on the persons tolerance level of the medication and supplement combined. The reason for this is because any type of medication treatment that is meant for treating the body from sicknesses and other life threatening illnesses can actually kill off the gut flora microorganisms that are in the intestines. This also includes the bacteria that helps make the Vitamin K that our bodies need by reducing the amount of what we absorb. This is why it is always best to talk to your physician or a dietitian before starting any type of intake of supplements.

A Vitamin K deficiency is caused by a long time use of medications. Using medication for an excessive period of time may cause issues with the gut flora microorganism bacteria, which could reduce the ability to clot blood.

Symptoms of a Vitamin E deficiency can include the following: bruising easily, skin problems, bleeding from the mouth, urinary and genital track problems, stomach disorders, and intestinal disorders.

It is also important for newborns to receive their first shot of the vitamin, because their own ability to manufacture the vitamin in the intestine can take at least one week to become present in the body. Without the shot, they would be at a high risk of developing a bleeding disorder called hemorrhagic disease. They must be able to get it by vaccine. They also need it so that it can help their blood clot if bleeding were ever to occur.

For adults, on the other hand, the best way to avoid developing a Vitamin K deficiency is to simply try not taking any medication for an excessive period of time.

A deficiency can occur in people with conditions that affect the absorptions of fats that come from the intestine, which is known as cystic fibrosis.

The daily requirement of Vitamin K should be 0.12 mg. If you much rather be getting your sources of Vitamin K from foods instead of supplements, then the best choices that you can find this source from are the following: apricots, asparagus, broccoli, Brussels sprouts, cabbage, carrots, celery, cauliflower, grapes, green peas, pears, plums and spinach.

These foods contain 0.01mg of Vitamin K per 1 ¾-7 oz (50-200g) serving.

However, please keep in mind that in order to make sure that you are getting an adequate amount of this vitamin, you would need to be eating at least 3-6 pieces of fruits and vegetables during the day. So, eat up!

VITAMIN PRESERVATION IN FOOD

As we all know, fruits and vegetables are good for the health and the body's functions in addition to tasting good. Over time, the vitamins in these foods start to depreciate when cooked. No matter how the process is done, vegetables do lose an amount of vitamins they contain.

The vitamin loss in content of vegetables usually starts off during their shelf life. When they go through both their shelf life and cooking process, there is a greater loss of vitamins, especially after being cooked at high temperatures.

The best time fruits and vegetables contain their highest peak of vitamins is when harvested ripe and eaten soon after without being processed. Common mistakes that are made are when some people choose to harvest a fruit or vegetable when premature and then letting them ripen, only to eat them soon after.

Another good option is frozen foods, such as fruits and vegetables, because when they are ripe and picked fresh, they are immediately frozen so that the nutrients are better preserved.

In order to make sure that the produce you buy in cans are going to remain fresh, you must store them properly for the prevention of nutrients, preferably in a dark cool place. This works best for produce because they contain Vitamin C and Vitamin B2 (riboflavin), which are both sensitive to light. When they are packaged and left in conditions like this, the vitamin content starts to degrade at high temperatures very quickly.

When cooking vegetables, remember that they should always be cooked for minimum amount of time. Do not boil them in a lot of water. Instead, you can either microwave or steam the vegetables in a little bit of water to better preserve the nutrients.

Steaming vegetables are better than boiling, because they prevent them from losing vitamins, minerals, and other important nutrients from being lost while boiling.

Getting your daily intake of vitamins doesn't necessarily mean that you can only get them in pill form. They can also be obtained from fruits, vegetables, and other healthy foods too.

Healthy foods can really make a big difference in a person's life, their daily activity by giving them more energy, and not only will they look good, but also feel good as well. By getting in an adequate amount of vitamins from fruit, vegetables, and other healthy foods, this will be able to provide the body with the right amount that it needs.

Chapter 14

The All Natural Way to Get Energy

Vitamin and minerals are essential for healthy living. So, what is the best way to get them? It's best to eat fresh whole foods, because not only are they good for you, but they have also been ripened by the sun. The sun also contains the most vitalizing energy.

Consider putting these naturally rich foods into your diet and see what a difference it can make in your life!

Grains

Some good grain choices are amaranth, basmati rice, oatmeal, and whole wheat.

Legumes

You can also try legumes, such as lentils, kidney beans, white beans, black-eyed peas, soy-milk, mug dale, tofu, and soybeans.

DAIRY

Dairy is another energy booster. Fresh yogurt, goat cheese and cottage cheese are good.

NUTS

Nuts are also high in protein, such as almonds, Brazil nuts, hazelnuts, pine nuts, pistachios, and walnuts.

NUT ENERGY SMOOTHIE RECIPE

If you're ever in the mood to try an energy drink, these 6 types of nuts should be able to do the trick instead. I prefer to use almonds because they are my favorite, and I enjoy putting them on my favorite treat: low-fat, creamy vanilla ice cream.

ALMOND MILK RECIPE

You can also use almonds to make almond milk. The best way to do this is to soak about 12 of them overnight. In the morning take them out, remove the skins, and then place the almonds in a blender. Add a cup of warm milk, a little cardamom powder, a little black pepper, and one tablespoon of honey. Then blend the mix up for about 5 minutes before enjoying. This energy drink is good for you, because almonds, milk, and honey are super rich in protein and will nourish and energize you.

VEGETABLES

Of course, a lot of us know that vegetables are good for the body, only because we've learned that at an early age. To some of us, that still doesn't matter.

I know that vegetables aren't exactly everyone's favorite, but, if prepared right, they will taste really good. The good thing about vegetables is that you can cook them any way you like. They also taste good when grilled and served with steak, shrimp, chicken, and rice. You should be eating at least 3 to 5 servings of veggies a day. Very few of us meet this mark and end up missing out on one of the most important ways of improving health and preventing diseases.

Vegetables are also excellent sources of Vitamin A, in the form of beta carotene. These two vitamins help keep your skin and eyes healthy and your bones strong. Also, they help fight infection. They also work with other vitamins and minerals to keep the muscles healthy.

Vegetables are an excellent source of folate and fiber. These two play an important role in the diet and also reduces your chances of having cardiovascular disease when a high fiber diet is kept normal.

Fiber also helps keep the intestinal tract working well and may help reduce the risk of colon cancer. A high fiber diet is also low in fat and can play a vital role in weight control.

Just remember, when cooking vegetables, you should use a good cooking method to minimize loss of nutrients.

Dried Fruits

Dried fruits come in many varieties, and they can be bought from just about any food store. However, if you already have fruit at home, you too can dry what you have in stock. The best way to do it would be to use a special fruit dehydrator. Dehydrating fruit never takes the nutrients away, and they are actually good for you. They contain more nutrients and calories then fresh fruits would have by weight.

Some fruits that are dried are often treated with sulfur dioxide so that their nutrients are better preserved. These fruits include apples, apricots, raisins, peaches, and pears. However, since some dried fruits are treated with sulfur dioxide, it can be a nuisance for people who suffer from asthma because of their sensitivity. They should always be a little more cautious when consuming dried fruits by choosing to eat an alternative that is not treated with sulfur dioxide.

One of the best things that make dried fruits so good is that they can either be eaten by themselves or added to a tasty dish, even added to baked treats too. Fruits are an excellent source of vitamins and minerals. They contain Vitamins A and C, fiber, and potassium. It is best to eat a mixture of all types of fruits to make sure that you are getting in the proper nutrition the body needs.

Apples

The skin of apples contains a good source of fiber, which is important for regulating normal bowel movements. Apples have at least 75 calories.

Apricots

These are good, but they are better when they are fresh. However, they are still healthy for you when dried or in the can. They contain about 9 calories.

Bananas

Surprisingly, most of us do not know this, but bananas are considered to be a type of herb and not a fruit. They contain 60 calories, and they are excellent sources of vitamins and minerals.

Blueberries

Blueberries are good for you, because they contain an excellent source of antioxidants that help to prevent the body from getting urinary tract infections. Blueberries contain around 75 calories.

CANTALOUPES

These are good for you, and they contain carotene that is a form of Vitamin A that can help the body fight cancer. Each slice of cantaloupe contains about 60 calories.

GRAPES

Not only are they delicious and good for you, but grapes are also an excellent source of vitamins and minerals. They contain 88 calories.

KIWI

This semi-prickly, fuzzy fruit contains 22 calories and, depending on the size, can contain different amounts of vitamins.

PEACHES

Just like any piece of fruit, they can be added to just about any dish or eaten by themselves. Peaches contain a good source of Vitamins A, C, D, and potassium. Depending on the size, a peach can contain 36 to 42 calories.

Pears

Each pear contains about 97 to 100 calories. It is best to buy them when they are not fully ripened so that you can enjoy them when they are ready to be eaten fresh.

Pineapple

Pineapples are good for helping the body to digest food better, while also helping to protect it from developing cardio vascular disease and helping the reduction of inflammation. Pineapple also has an enzyme called bromeliad. Pineapples contain 70 calories.

Plums

Plums are an excellent source of Vitamins A, C, and potassium. They also contain 34 calories.

Raisins

Raisins are very nutritional and can help to deliver a good source of energy to the body so that you are able to get through the day. They are also good with dried, unsalted almonds. The problem is, when eaten by themselves, they can contain a lot of sugar, so limit the intake amount.

Raspberries

These bite-sized morsels can come in roughly around 100 different varieties. This type of fruit is very fragile and expensive to buy, which explains why they are sold in small, clear packages. Raspberries contain 60 calories when eaten by the cup.

Watermelon

This Godzilla-sized mega fruit is extremely delicious and good for you. They also make a perfect treat to have for hot summer days or even good for completing a fruit salad. One cup of watermelon alone can contain 55 calories, and it is an excellent source of vitamins and minerals.

Some fruits in general can contain more vitamins and minerals than others, which is why it is extremely important to eat a great variety.

The Top 15 Healthy Whole Foods

In addition to the above mentioned foods. Here are the Top 15 foods that are good for helping to prevent diseases, keeping you healthy by giving you nutrients and energy.

1.) Blueberries

They contain Vitamins B, C, and fiber. They also contain flavanoids, which help to make the circulation of blood in the body and help it defend itself against nasty infections that can lead to health complications later on down the line.

2.) Broccoli

Broccoli is high in vitamins and minerals, definitely rich in Vitamin C and beta carotene. Broccoli even contains folate. Folic acids are good for helping to protect the body from cancers and cardiovascular disease.

3.) Flaxseed

You should never leave out flaxseed, which is a form of fatty acids that are rich in Omega-3's. Omega-3 fatty acid is good for treating high cholesterol and high blood pressure.

4.) Legumes

Legumes are also good because they contain fiber for helping to lower cholesterol levels. However, legumes must be eaten on a regular basis. They are rich in iron, potassium, and folate.

5.) Almonds

Almonds, specifically, out of all the different varieties of nuts, contain more nutrients, which also makes them a good source of Vitamin E, protein, and selenium.

Nuts can also help to lower cholesterol. They are high in Vitamin E and selenium. Nuts also share the job of reducing high blood pressure.

6.) Fat-free Yogurt

Besides all the many different tasty varieties, fat-free yogurt is also a good source to obtain calcium from. Just like milk is important for promoting healthy bones and teeth, yogurt does the same and contains protein.

7.) Oily Fish

In addition to a food that is high in protein, oily fish, such as trout, salmon, tuna, and mackerel are other perfect choices of foods that are rich in this nutrient and also are good sources of Omega-3 fatty acid, which can also help to control cholesterol levels.

8.) Olive Oil

This is a much better oil to use. Over all the other cooking oils, it is the healthiest for you and contains good monounsaturated fats, which can help maintain the levels of promoting good cholesterol.

9.) Quinoa

Although it is a type of grain, quinoa is not something to be taken lightly. This is a grain that is able to do wonders for the body by promoting health. It has no gluten, and it is high in protein and fiber, which is also known to be part of the Andean diet. One other important fact about this grain is that it comes from South America.

10.) Oatmeal

Oatmeal is another excellent source of fiber, which is good for helping to lower blood cholesterol levels. Oatmeal also contains magnesium and zinc. Try using the plain, steel cut variety instead of the flavored kinds.

Just remember, the next time you happen to see a commercial advertisement on how good oatmeal is in helping to improve health, you should take that message seriously. Believe it or not, they are not kidding.

11.) Red Grapes

Yes, red grapes are deliciously sweet, and they are nature's gift for us to enjoy. There is a reason why they are so good.

They contain antioxidants that help to protect the body from developing cancers.

12.) Oranges

Although it is crucial that you take in plenty of antioxidants, fiber, and Omega-3 fatty acids, it is also important to include Vitamin C into the picture, which makes oranges the perfect candidates for making this source obtainable.

Vitamin C is good for the prevention of the free radicals from damaging the tissues and cells.

13.) Peppers

Not just any peppers, but bell peppers are an excellent source of Vitamin C and contain beta—carotene, which are considered to be antioxidants and can help fight off cancers.

14.) Spinach

Yes, the leafy green vegetable may not make you look like Popeye right away, but, realistically, it sure will make you healthier later on down the line. Spinach is rich in folate, iron, lutein and Vitamin E. It also contains antioxidant properties as well.

15.) Tomatoes

Alongside all the cancer fighting foods, tomatoes are another source that are rich in antioxidants and lycopene. The best way to make sure that you don't lose the source of lycopene through tomatoes is to cook them in olive oil.

Not only will these foods give you tons of energy, they'll make you look and feel better, too. And, after all, that's what it's all about: getting energy and staying healthy!

CHAPTER 15

YOUR WEEKLY GUIDE TO HEALTHY EATING

STAY STRONG ALL WEEK LONG

It isn't easy to stay loyal to eating clean seven days a week. Maybe it's easier for you to eat clean Monday through Friday, but you want to splurge on the weekends. In a way, I do have to admit that this is very understandable. After all, the average person does work really hard all week, and they expect to be able to rest on the weekends before resuming work mode on Monday.

Although this is true for the mindset of work, the same thing goes for eating clean. As soon as Friday hits, you begin to abandon the thoughts of sticking to a healthy diet for hanging out with friends and start off with greasy foods that you wouldn't normally eat on the weekdays. By Saturday, your desire for more junk worsens, causing you to convince yourself that whatever you decide to splurge on, it won't even be that much, and you can start fresh on Monday.

What makes it worse is that this normally happens when you are out at the mall shopping with either friends or family. And malls do have food courts with lots of restaurants advertising and cooking so much food that it is just too hard for one's nose to ignore. And that is when the temptation to commit another food sins hits, turning you into the Tazmanian Food Devil, whirling through the food court from line to line, until you finally make up your mind on what you want to eat. The sad thing is, the sin of eating junk food at the food court sometimes doesn't stop there. The bad behavior may even carry on until that night.

By Sunday, it all begins to set in as you get lazy by hanging out on your couch, finishing off the last day of the weekend with chips and dips. By then all the guilt starts to set in, making you realize that all of the weekend binging you've been doing has ruined your whole week's worth of healthy eating. By the time you have realized how guilty you are, it's already too late. The damage is done, which means its back to square one on Monday. But only to promise yourself that you won't do that again. As soon as Friday comes back around, all promises are broken.

Let's face it, we have all been through this scenario, which is common among a lot of eat clean fans. So don't hate yourself over it. If you know how to eat clean on the weekdays and also want to eat whatever you want on the weekends, then go for it. There is absolutely no reason why you should feel guilty.

If you don't have the hang of it just yet, here are some tips to help you.

Tip #1: Keep your cabinets stocked with healthy foods.

Always begin at home by not loading up your cabinets with snacks that are unhealthy or any foods that are high in calories. Always keep both fresh fruits and vegetables, low-fat cheeses, whole grain crackers, and other foods and nutritious snacks that won't harm your calorie intake.

Tip #2: Eat a healthy breakfast.

Of course, you know by now not to skip breakfast. If you have been good all week, then continue on throughout Saturday and Sunday by having a breakfast that has an adequate amount of protein and fiber, like eggs, low-fat dairy products, whole grain cereal, or peanut butter with whole grain toast and a nice cold glass of orange juice.

Tip #3: Create a food journal.

As crazy as this may sound, if you feel the need to record your progress, then don't be afraid to. Keep a small note pad and treat it like a food diary by writing various ways to keep yourself motivated to keep eating healthy and keep track of all the foods that you eat.

Tip #4: Read the labels.

Look at all the labels of everything you want to eat. If the fat and calories content are high enough to mess up your diet, stay away from it.

Tip #5: Reward yourself.

Once you have been good on your diet all week, then you can reward yourself with a little bit of whatever your treat is for that week. The trick is, though, to eat low calories all week so that when you do have that cheat meal, it won't harm your diet.

Tip #6: Fill up on fruits and veggies.

Above all, just remember to eat lots of fruits and vegetables, because these are low in calories, high in fiber, and very nutritious. When you eat a lot of fiber, it keeps you full.

Tip #7: Eat before going out.

Be very careful when you go shopping. Before you go out, try to eat a very nutritious meal, especially if you are going out to the mall. Most restaurants tend to serve food in large portions, so a smart thing to do choose small entrées, or food such as soup, salad, or an appetizer. If you happen to order a meal, thinking that it is small but you still have leftovers, save the rest for the next day.

EATING HEALTHY EVERYDAY

Here is an example of clean foods to eat daily, ranging from breakfast to dinner. This type of meal regimen is only an example to show you what foods are good for you for energy and fat burning.

Day 1

Breakfast:

Whole grain muffin
3 slices of low-fat deli turkey
1 slice of 1% cheddar cheese
Brunch:
Grilled kofta kebabs
1 lb extra lean ground beef
2 tbsp fresh thyme leaves
1 tbsp crushed chili peppers
1 slice of lemon
4 pinches of salt for added taste
2 pinches of black pepper
1 tbsp fresh parsley leaves skewer sticks

Lunch:

Ham rolls
12 slices of low-fat ham
¼ cup of low-fat PHILLIDELPIA cream cheese
1 cup of broccoli
Afternoon Snack:
1 scoop of casein protein
1 cup of blueberries
Evening Snack:
1 scoop of whey protein
1 scoop of casein protein

23 haribu gummi bears

DINNER:

Chicken wheat tortilla wrap
1 chopped chicken breast
1 medium whole wheat tortilla
2 tbsp of reduced fat mild cheddar cheese
1 small cup of black beans
1 small cup of white rice
2 tbsp of salsa

DAY 2

BREAKFAST:

4 egg whites and 2 whole eggs
1 whole grain bagel
2 scoops of natural peanut butter
1 tall glass of orange juice

BRUNCH:

Turkey waldorf salad
1 skinless turkey breast cut to small cubes
2 cups of chopped celery
1 cup of chopped red apple
½ cup of sliced chopped onion

½ cup of walnuts

½ cup of chopped cilantro

1 slice of freshly squeezed lemon juice

4 pinches of salt for added taste

2 pinches of black pepper

1 cup of 1% American cheese bits

Lunch:

6 oz of deli turkey slices

2 cups of green salad

1 tbsp of vinegar dressing

1 scoop of casein protein drink on the side

Afternoon Snack:

1 cup of well chopped pineapples

1 scoop of whey protein drink on the side

Evening Snack:

The lean burger

1 lean ground beef patty

1 slice of fat-free American cheese

1 cup of well chopped lettuce

½ slice of onion

2 teaspoons of fat-free mayonnaise

1 whole grain burger bun

2 slices of tomato

Dinner:

Grilled salmon filet

Brown rice

Steamed mixed vegetables

Small side salad

Small cup of fat-free Italian dressing

1 tall cup of unsweetened iced tea or water

1 cup of strawberries

Day 3

Breakfast:

1 small bowl of plain fat-free yogurt

1 cup of granola bits

1 small side bowl of whole grain cereal with 1% milk

Brunch:

Fat-free turkey burger

1 cup of cereal flakes

½ cup of skim milk

4 pinches of salt for added taste

Chicken bouillon

1 slice of well chopped onion

3 egg whites

1 lb of lean ground turkey

1 whole wheat or whole grain burger

Lunch:

Taco salad

1 lb of ground beef

1 small bag of taco seasoning

1 small cup of water to mix with

7 cups of shredded roman lettuce

1 can of corn

2 slices of tomatoes

1 18 oz bottle of low-fat Italian dressing

2 cups of large natural tortilla chips

Afternoon Snack:

Protein drink

1 scoop of whey protein

1 small bowl of oatmeal

Evening Snack:

1 stick of low-fat string cheese

2 oz of trail mix

Dinner:

Classic grilled chicken salad

2 chopped grilled chicken breast

1 half slice of medium green pepper

1 half sliced medium onion

1 sliced medium tomato

½ cup of small black olives

½ cup of grated mozzarella cheese

½ cup of fat-free vinegar dressing

Day 4

Breakfast:

5 scrambled egg whites

1 whole egg

1 piece of whole wheat toast

1 medium banana

1 cup 1% milk

Brunch:

Grilled Oregano Chicken Skewers

28 oz of chicken breast

1 tbsp of mustard

1 tbsp of olive oil

5 well chopped pieces of garlic

2 tbsp of oregano

1 tbsp of cumin

4 pinches of salt for added taste

2 pinches of black pepper

½ slice of well chopped onion skewer sticks for the cooked chicken

Lunch:

Lean turkey sandwich

4 lean deli turkey slices

2 slices of tomato

2 slices of whole wheat bread

2 spoons of fat-free mayonnaise

1 slice of fat-free American cheese

Afternoon Snack:

Protein drink

1 scoop of casein protein

1 large apple

Evening Snack:

10 celery sticks

1 small side cup of fat-free Philadelphia cream cheese

½ cup of chopped olives

1 tall glass of 1% milk

Dinner:

Lean steak dinner

1 12 oz piece of steak

1 large baked potato

15 medium sized cooked shrimp and peeled

2 pinches of black pepper

3 pinches of MRS dash

4 pinches of salt for added taste

1 slice of well chopped onion

1 whole chopped garlic

1 piece of chopped ginger

1 cup of plain salsa sauce

Mix the together to create your own shrimp cocktail sauce

Day 5

Breakfast:

1 medium bowl of oat meal
6 egg whites
1 protein shake
1 scoop of whey
1 scoop of casein
1 spoon of flaxseed oil

Brunch:

Grilled tuna steak
18 oz steak tuna
1 slice of freshly squeezed lemon juice
1 tbsp of olive oil
4 pinches of salt for added taste
2 pinches of black pepper
1 cup of mixed veggies

Lunch:

12 whole wheat crackers
3 sticks of mozzarella string cheese
1 oz of walnuts

Afternoon Snack:

Protein drink
1 scoop of casein protein
1 medium banana

Evening Snack:

Protein drink
1 scoop of whey protein
1 scoop of casein protein
1 large slice of angel food cake

Dinner:

Thai beef stew
1 tbsp of olive oil
1/3 of chopped lean sirloin steak
½ of beef stew seasoning mix
1 can of mixed veggies
1 can of low sodium beef broth
1/3 cup of teddy's natural peanut butter with sodium